- Weighing Love -
By: Paula Galli

BURMAN BOOKS

MEDIA CORP.

Published by BurmanBooks Media Corp.
260 Queens Quay West
Suite 1102
Toronto, Ontario
Canada M5J 2N3

Cover design: Lara Vanderheide
Interior design: Lara Vanderheide
Editing: Anna Watson

Distribution:
TruMedia Group LLC
575 Prospect Street, Suite 301
Lakewood, NJ 08701
ISBN 978-1-927005-37-8
Printed and bound in The United States of America

Dedication

Weighing Love is dedicated to anyone who believes that they are not good enough, worthy enough or truly perfect, inside and out, just as they currently are. This book was written to show you that just as you need to put time and effort into making a relationship work with a spouse, family member or friend, that same time and effort, if not more, needs to be spent with yourself in order to ensure that relationship is strong, vital and authentic.

- Weighing Love -
Table of Contents

Acknowledgements

I would first like to thank and recognize my amazing parents. Dad and Mom, without your constant support throughout my life I would have never been able to get where I am today. Thank-you for truly listening to me, especially over the last few years, and for believing in my dreams, one of them being writing this book. It means a lot to know that you have always been rooting for me. I love you both so much.

Trish, my amazing sister. Words cannot even begin to express how grateful I am to have you in my life. Without you I don't know where I would be today. You have not only been a sister but a friend and so much more. Thank-you for always believing in me and being by my side no matter what.

I would also like to acknowledge my Nonni Galli, Nonni Mantia, who are no longer with us, and my god parents Uncle Ori and Auntie Joanne. You have all played such an important role in my life – thank-you for supporting me and loving me unconditionally.

To my extended family members – both those who are actual blood relatives and those who are not – there are too many of you to list off, but you all know who you are! I am so blessed to have such a big family who truly cares about one another and has everyone's best interest at heart.

I would also like to personally thank some of my girl-friends/sisters from different mothers!

Kyla – you are truly my soulmate, my sister and my best friend. You are the other half of my tree – or whatever that monk said to us in Singapore! Our life-long friendship has been such a pivotal part of my life. Without you, I am not sure if I would be who I am.

Stephanie – more than twenty years later you are still my girl. Having you in my life as one of my sisters has been so important and meaningful to me. I know that no matter where life takes us I can always count on you for your constant support and a listening ear, our sisterhood means so much to me.

Natalie – you entered my life when ED was at his worst. Without you as my friend, the person I admired through those years and my counselor in a sense – I SERIOUSLY don't know if I would have been strong enough to make all of the beneficial decisions I made since I have met you. You will forever hold a spe-cial place in my heart and I don't say it enough but THANK-YOU so much for everything you have done for me.

Isabel – our friendship has been such a meaningful part of my life. It was just yesterday we met on the playground and began doing "our walk" down the high school halls! I know that I can always count on you to listen to what I have to say and you have my best interest at heart, I love you so much.

Milena – our friendship was extremely close for those years when ED was living in full force. If I look back I am not sure if I would have survived without our friendship, so thank-you for putting up with all of my dysfunction. Since then things have certainly changed, as things in life do, but no matter where life takes us you know that I will always love you and have your best interests at heart and I know the same goes for you to me. Xo Gelina

Liz – no matter where our life takes us we always end up back together sharing similar viewpoints and out-looks on life, spirituality and healing. We have a special connection that started years back and continues today. I will never forget those nights in high school hanging out in your room, or passing notes to each other at the office and our days by the water – both then and now. I am so happy you are in my life Betty, your constant support and encouragement means more than you know.

Sarah – over the last few years our friendship has gotten so much closer and having your constant support, acceptance and belief in me has been so important to my growth, development and life. You are an amazing person and I am so blessed to have you in my life. Thanks for always having my best interests at heart and believing in my dreams.

Renee – you and I lived together through my first two years away from home. Those years forever shaped my life and changed it, for it was throughout that time that I began to break free from ED. Thank-you for always being there for me whenever I needed a shoulder to cry on or a listening ear about any and everything that comes up. I am so grateful that Steam Heat brought us together all those years ago!

I seriously wouldn't have been able to get through all of this without having each of you in my life. You have all played such important roles in helping me become the woman that I am.

With that being said, there are so many other important people that have been a huge part of my life. I could write an entire book thanking each of you, but since I can't I just wanted to acknowledge you. I hope you each know your importance to me.

Yola K, Amara K, Lisa L, Nao H, Petra S, Marta P, Danielle L, Martin O, Dustin P, Ted S, David F, Justin S, Sharon G, Gleb G, Anthony H, Giuditta G, Kelli T, Adrian B, Stephanie S, Shanda S, & Nicole M– again you have each have played a special role throughout different parts of my life that have been extremely meaningful and important to me. There are SO many more of you that I can thank and I hope you know who you are – if not I will tell you to your face!

Nicci and Piotr thank-you for the beautiful pictures in this book – they added such a warm touch!

To all of my lemons: Leandra, Nick, Lisa, Pam(s), Kaya, Courtney, Christine, Lianne, Lindsay, Amanda, Martin, Nicola, Angela, Ashley and the rest of you - you know who you are! Our time together at lululemon forever changed my life, the book is finally finished!!! Thanks for believing in me and allowing me to be the Goal Coach to all of you!

To all of my dance girls and guys, throughout the years, like Maija, Alicia, Amanda, Tina, Kira and the rest of you from STM, ESD, & OHDC, our times together played a big role in becoming who I am, so thank-you for your friendship, love and support.

To my other St. Greg's girls: Andrea, Allison, Aviva, Helena, Steph, Victoria, Sar, Heather, Gianna, Nadia, Katie - our times together have shaped my life in extremely meaningful ways that unless you are a St. Greg's girl you will not understand. Even though our lives have grown apart we will always share a special bond – "friends are like flowers - here at St. Gregs!"

To all of my colleagues from The Institute Of Holistic Nutrition: Jen R, Jen W, Sondi, Rachelle, Barbara, Shayna, Sherry, Jason, Joanne & everyone else from our year – our time together was an extremely important part of my healing and growth – thanks for all of your support and love.

Lastly, I would like to specially recognize Kyla F and Jennifer O. When I was first breaking free from ED, both of you played as important mentors, as well as, role models for the woman I always wanted to be. You each helped me transition out of ED in different ways by allowing me to see that I could become whoever I wanted to be. Thank-you from the bottom of my heart for not only helping me through my ED but for believing in me. It helped me learn how to truly believe in myself.

The Intention Of This Book

This book was written with the intention of ultimately helping you fall in love with yourself, your body and your life through breaking free from ED (Eating Disorder) or any other dysfunctional relationship or connection that you have in your life.

For those of you who are choosing to break free from ED, it is a brave choice. I want you to acknowledge the power and strength you already have by just picking up this book. I also want to forewarn you that through this process of breaking free from ED and re-discovering who you truly are, there are going to be some uncomfortable feelings that may come along the way. Just remember that oftentimes in order to have breakthroughs like breaking free from ED, going through uncomfortable feelings often fueled by fears and uncertainty, is usually a necessary part of the process.

Just remember that those feelings are your fears and *not reality*. They are only uncomfortable feelings and you can push through them; they will become comfortable feelings as you move yourself out of your comfort zone and reach the other side: acceptance.

I promise you that this will all start to make more

sense while you are going through this process.

Last, I want you to know that breaking free from ED, personal transformation and re-discovering who you are, is a journey that takes time. Please be patient with yourself, compassionate when you fall, and find the courage and strength that you have right now – the courage that allowed you to choose to want to read this book in the first place – to pick you back up again.

It is also very important to know that when we are in the process of changing and transforming into who we really are, we can and most likely will "slip up" by making a "mistake" such as falling back into old behaviors and patterns. This is a completely normal part of the transformational process. When this happens you can label yourself as being a failure and oftentimes it may feel like you want to give up on even trying to change.

We may even convince ourselves that we are not capable or deserving of being anybody different or having a different life, because we messed up. I am here to tell you that this couldn't be further from the truth. Changing behaviors takes time and it is only normal that a slip up here and there will occur throughout the process.

It is at those times that you have the opportunity to pick yourself back up and continue working towards your goal, whatever that may be. Remember that the most successful people have all "failed" many times before they made it to the top of their game.

I say, let's change the lens upon which we label and see the word "failure" and rather call it an "opportunity for learning more about ourselves." It is through these learning opportunities that we gain valuable life experiences, which in turn allow us to grow more and more into who we truly are. It's extremely beneficial to keep these types of thoughts in mind while you're going through the process of personal transformation and re-discovery.

I have almost said everything I feel I need to say to you before you begin to read this book. I do suggest that you read through this book once. Then slowly read it again, only this time, do each of the exercises. Give yourself the amount of time needed to work through each exercise, without holding any judgments or expectations.

Just a few last thoughts before we begin:

(1) NOW is YOUR time to begin your journey in breaking free from ED. You wouldn't have

picked up this particular book on this particular day if it wasn't meant to be any other way. I believe that we attract whatever we are truly asking for in our lives, and for some reason this book has landed in your hand today.

(2) NOW is YOUR time to begin your journey of re-discovering who you are through personal transformation. This is the reason why you are reading this book today.

(3) NOW is YOUR time to begin your journey of learning how to truly fall in love with yourself, your body and your life by becoming your own best friend.

ED may try to tell you differently along the way, but I am here to tell you that
YOU are *worthy* and *deserving* of all of this.
This is my intention for YOU.

Introduction

As I lay in my bed I looked around. My bedroom was no longer perfect like it used to be, it was a mess. It was a disaster. It was disgusting. There was absolutely no more love left in my room. My mirror was covered with self-hatred and self-doubt. My closet was filled with lies. My bed was filled with betrayal and lack of love. My pillow was soaked with sadness. Pain. Fear. My walls were smeared with guilt and regret. My curtains were covered in embarrassment and shame. My once perfect, pink and purple bedroom was no longer there. It was no longer there. Just like I was gone, my bedroom had disappeared too and manifested into something else. Something possessed by demons. ED had taken over, yet I had no idea.

This night was different, much different than any other night prior to it. I knew that I had taken my final straw. I knew that I needed to make a change in my life because I was now twenty years old. Turning twenty was a big reality kick in the ass for me.

If you look back to pictures of that night any outsider would think that I had a great twentieth birthday party. My boyfriend and all my friends were there. I was wearing a crown for heaven's sake.

But behind that big smile that I always had on in public, I was crying inside. I felt fat. I felt stupid. I felt unloved. I felt lost. I felt really alone.

In my life there are a certain amount of times that I will have to do something; there is a certain amount of pain I let myself endure before I hit my version of rock bottom. My rock bottom is probably similar to most of yours, a lot lower than some of yours and possibly a lot higher than others. One way or another I would usually hit the ground so hard that my face would look completely deformed once I stood up. I would wake up and look in the mirror, completely unable to recognize my very own reflection; I was no longer myself.

He and I were both done with this relationship yet neither of us had the guts to officially end it. I smoked a lot of weed that night, hoping that maybe it wouldn't make me be paranoid and more insecure of everything around me then when I was sober. Wrong.

I drank a lot thinking that would be the answer to becoming happier. Wrong. And then I did one more thing that night, which I had never done before – cocaine.

Happy Fucken Birthday Paula!!!

In my mind doing that one line of cocaine meant that I had officially given up on the person I thought I was going to be when I was a little girl. All the dreams I had created for myself were officially thrown out the door. I didn't know who I was, what I was, what I was doing or where I was going in life.

The next morning I knew it was over. I knew things had to change because that wasn't who I was; that wasn't who I wanted to be. I came home a complete mess, fully knowing that was my last night of trying to keep doing what I had been doing year in and year out with my relationship, with myself and with my life in general.

I remembered hearing that the definition of insanity is when someone tries to do the same thing over and over again and expecting a different result to emerge. I guess at that point you could have called me insane because I was pretty much living my life in that exact manner. Doing the same things day-in and day-out hoping for different outcomes to take place.

I was living inside of a world filled with constant misery.

Actually, I was living inside of two different worlds.

Reality and fantasy land. Reality was ultimately filled with pain and a fantasy land, which I had created to cope with reality, was only occurring within my mind. My fantasy world is what kept me putting up with all the misery that I was enduring throughout my reality. Not only within my on-again, off-again, almost four year relationship, but in regards to my life as a whole.

My dream that we would one day wake up and be this different couple, these different people kept me clinging to him. Like a leech sucking blood out of a humans flesh I couldn't let go of the thought of 'us'. To the thought of what we once were. I needed to try harder right? I needed to give us a chance *just one last time*. The thing is, is that this *just one last time* occurred about 27831721893 times before that, always with the same outcome.

We would always engage in the same conversation. We would exchange our devotion and love for one another by stating how we would both try to be better, which would last for maybe a week, two tops. That would always be followed by a few weeks of pure bullshit, which would cause me to want to end it; but I couldn't get past that *just one last time* mentality.

It wasn't only in my romantic relationship that I was living out this *just one last time* mentality; it was also expressed within my relationship with food, my body and myself. I would engage in binges, weeks at a time, usually that coincided with the flow of my relationship.

Other times it would be expressed the opposite way as well. ED had a mind of his own where he would either punish me for being too happy or console me when I was feeling sad. I was living in a black and white world filled with high and lows, a completely yes and no city.

If my relationship was going well, ED was controlling me to be 'good' by trying to eat like a 'normal person' which in ED's mind, meant dieting. Other times, he would punish me for being happy, for having a good day, by making me go to bed hating myself for my lack of self-control with food that night when he forced me to scarf down 4000 calories in one sitting, at 1 am mind you.

ED also didn't hide himself from me during my weeks of hell with my boyfriend. He would disguise himself as some sort of doctor who spoke to me like he knew the right medicine which would make me feel better.

Truthfully all ED was, was a very uneducated anesthesiologist who only knew one thing, how to numb me.

ED's medical plan prescribed that I engage in additional self-mutilation by stuffing my face day after day until the pain from my stomach outweighed the pain that was pounding through my ever exploding chest and mind. When I felt nauseous each morning and had irregular bowel movements I knew ED's medication was working. Usually after a week of late night binging, he would incorporate some special teas, liquids or pills to help flush out all the excess toxins which were originally numbing but always caused my hips to stretch, my belly to bulge and my ass to expand.

A few tablespoons of mineral oil would sometimes do the trick or some diet pills would work too. But that seemed wrong, that seemed like I had an eating disorder or something and God knows I was smarter than that. I once tried throwing up and I remember sitting over the toilet with my fingers down my throat and the only thought that came to my mind was, *"Paula you are not bulimic, you don't have an eating disorder, get up and go to your room."*

That's how ED manipulated me, by telling me I was not one of 'those' people. Due to the fact that ED's prescription did not involve toilets or not eating, I did not believe I was engaging in any behavior that was really harmful, physically or psychologically.

I now know that's completely and utterly untrue.

ED became the spokesperson for my new love in life, Diet Teas. I could eat whatever I wanted and ED convinced me that it would erase all the calories eight hours later as they came streaming from my ass. So I guess ED did incorporate a toilet into his prescription after all, yet because it was coming from my behind rather than my front I didn't think there was a problem. That's how normal people go to the washroom. So I was just having some fun the night before and adding in some assistance with the release. That's normal right? Wrong.

I wanted to lose twenty pounds so this is what people do when they want to lose weight right? Wrong. But that's what ED convinced me to believe and let me tell you he is the most manipulative son of a bitch I've ever met, so I always believed him.

Let's get back to that night. Since I was twenty now, I felt that I could no longer waste any time. I did not want to wake up at twenty-five and still be sitting in the same place that I was sitting at when I was eighteen. I knew I wanted more. I knew I had to try, but where the heck did I begin?

When it comes to everything in my life, I write to

express, to figure out, to explore, to tap into my soul. So I grabbed a piece of paper and a pen and just began to watch my insides unfold. I will not go into details of the letter I wrote that night as it has no importance to my story but the overall theme was related to me knowing that I needed to leave, to get out, to move forward.

I had written countless letters just like this one up until this period so my boyfriend probably didn't even notice the big difference in this one. However, this letter was streaming from a much deeper and truer place than I had ever written from before. This shift was completely related to the search I was on for finding my true self. I had been on this search since the young age of nine, although I didn't even realize it. Completely and utterly unconscious. Completely unaware.

I wanted to find my way out of this maze which was my life, out of ED's Haunted House. I was searching for myself, one with real freedom, self-love, self-expression and independence. Even though I didn't really know if I would ever achieve this, I knew that I needed to at least try.

Just like always, whenever I would make such a bold decision, there would be two voices conversing inside my head. I now realize one was ED's voice and the other was my true self talking.

I didn't know this that night. For some reason though, I chose to listen to the voice which had been suppressed inside of me for so long now; it was so loud now that it was screaming to me at the top of its lungs; *"Paula, how much longer are you going to treat yourself like this? How much longer are you going to put your life, your dreams, your inspirations second for a relationship you aren't even sure fits you properly? How in heaven's name are you going to be able to be with someone if you don't know who you even are? How is it possible that you can contribute anything to a relationship with another human being if you are not even sure whose reflection you are looking at when you look in the mirror? How are you going to ever truly love somebody the way that you want and receive that love in return, if you don't even love yourself? How? Why? When are you going to put your foot down and change?"*

That voice had spoken to me for years now. I just ignored it. Well actually fear, denial and uncertainty caused me to ignore it, not to mention ED's confusing manipulative games.

That night, however, my true self could no longer hide from me anymore. For some reason I couldn't put it under the blanket, shove it under the rug, stuff it in the closet or lock it in a box. This voice was oozing out of every inch of my body, dripping from my nose, pouring from my sweat, salivating from my mouth.

It was now unavoidable. It was not only taking a stand but it was doing so with purpose, determination, and motivation. Somehow fear, denial, uncertainty and ED took a back seat that night, which I am so grateful for because if they had been sitting in the driver's seat like they had always been up until this point, who knows where I would be today.

*

March 14.2006
Today is my birthday; I am now twenty years old. This is the first day of a new time in my life where I should let go of all my teenage insecurities and try to look and move forward as a mature young woman. I recognize the fact that there are many things which I want to fix and improve about myself and within my life, but that if they don't change all at once or even right away when I try and things don't work out the way I want them to, I can always try again.

*

Eating Disorders have particular stereotypes around them. Just as I did, many people assume that because they are not hunched over a toilet bowl and they're not super skinny to the point where they need to be hospitalized, that they do not in fact have an Eating Disorder.

I know some of you didn't pick up this book because you believe you have an Eating Disorder. Some of you might have. Some of you may be turned off from this book already because the whole term Eating Disorder is making you feel like you cannot relate to the information that I am going to present to you.
I invite all of you to give this book a chance by beginning to understand why I am presenting the term Eating Disorder within this first paragraph.

The DSM (*Diagnostic Statistical Manual*) is a book that Psychologists and Psychiatrists use in order to label, categorize, identify and diagnose individuals with particular disorders. Eating Disorders are found within this book and amongst them there are specific categories depicting each particular diagnosis. If an individual fits into one of these categories as they're outlined, they can be given that specific diagnosis. Similarly, if they do not fit into any of these categories then they would not receive a diagnosis. You may be asking yourself, "What happens to those people who do not fit into the box as decided by whoever wrote the DSM? Does that mean they are not worthy of receiving care and attention for treatment for their unhealthy relationship with food and their bodies?"

In some cases, yes, this is very true.

This is the kind of real-world context through which most people see Eating Disorders. I am not saying that the DSM is entirely wrong, incorrect or something I do not believe. What I am saying, however, is that from my experience of being a young female with lots of female friends, I feel the term Eating Disorder needs to have a broader spectrum of symptoms and behaviors associated with it. We need to look at it through a different lens.

The truth is:
- Eating Disorders affect individuals of all shapes and sizes.
- Eating Disorders affect individuals who do not even believe they have an Eating Disorder.
- Eating Disorders affect even those who may seem the most unlikely to be living with one.

I know this because I lived it. I never thought I had an Eating Disorder.

Well I shouldn't say never. There was one time in my late teens where I remember crying hysterically to my boyfriend at the time and his mother, shouting, "I think I have an Eating Disorder!" over and over. Yet, nothing ever came from this seeming revelation because the truth was I wasn't super skinny, I wasn't hunched over a toilet bowl and because everything else seemed to be *normal* in my life, I felt that what-ever I was going through emotionally during that time was a result of the fact that I was having a hard time losing twenty pounds.

Those twenty pounds, those four extra sizes that I thought I needed to shrink, kept me locked inside of a prison, a prison that lay within my mind. A prison that was filled with rights and wrongs, good and bads, black and whites, and all or nothings. A prison that had me become completely disconnected from my body, food and lastly myself, so much that all I could focus my energy on was the shape and size of my body. The number on the scale. The number of calo-ries I ate. The number of calories I burned. The plan I had to follow in order to attain the right numbers, the right size and the perfection of my body.

I was a young girl growing up in the 90s, living in a relatively big city, where fashion images surrounded me, television shows promoted this idea of perfection and all of my friends were also overly concerned about the shape and size of their bodies. This to me was normal. Completely and utterly normal.

It wasn't until my forth year at university when I was studying psychology and reading about Eating Disorders in my textbook that the reality of my situation hit me. What I had considered to be normal up until this point was no longer seen as normality, but something much more extreme.

Even though the specific categories outlined for Eating Disorders that I was reading about did not perfectly relate to anything that I was currently doing, there was certainly an overlap. I would say that about 90% of my behaviors and actions at this time were in complete alliance with one of the particular Eating Disorder categorizes.

Yet, if I were to go to a typical treatment center that only helped individuals who fit the categories completely, I would have not received any treatment, because I wasn't "sick enough" in a sense. It is no kidding that many individuals who are dealing with issues around weight, their bodies and food live in silence and do not communicate how they are truly feeling out of fear of being rejected or ridiculed that there is nothing "wrong" with them as a result of not being "sick enough".

The ironic thing is that when I went to go get help for my eating disorder my own mind convinced me that I wasn't "sick enough" to even get help. I work with many clients, who express the same idea.

What I have learned is that feeling of not being "sick enough" occurs because of two reasons. One is the effect of living in a world that has stereotypical ideas around what Eating Disorders are. Add to that the fact that people living with Eating Disorders often don't even believe they have an Eating Disorder; their mind convinces them otherwise.

The truth of the matter is that Eating Disorders can occur on a broader spectrum of behaviors and symptoms.

The Eating Disorder that I had did not disrupt my ability to participate in life, though it did affect it. I definitely wasn't at the end degree where I needed to be hospitalized as I was still able to go to school, participate in extracurricular activities, eat food and hang out with my friends. My weight was viewed as *normal* and because of that no one would ever think just by looking at me, that my relationship with my body, food and myself were extremely dysfunctional and unhealthy.

I think because no one said anything, I just assumed that thinking this way was once again *normal*. When I lost those twenty pounds everything else would fix itself for the better. Boy was I wrong. For over a decade of my life I lived this way and thought this way. A decade too long.

This is why I wanted to write this book, to help you from spending any more of your precious time being preoccupied with food, your body and the way that you look. This is why I have dedicated my entire career around this, because I know firsthand what it feels like to truly not feel comfort in your own skin. In this book, I would like to introduce you to ED and re-educate you about what Eating Disorders are and the spectrum that I believe is associated with them, ranging from mild-moderate-high.

All of the views expressed in this book are culled from my own experience both professionally and personally.

Let me be clear in telling you what this book is NOT about. This book isn't about trying to fit yourself into a box – not even on the spectrum of whether you feel that you have an Eating Disorder or not. Nowhere in this book do I delve into this spectrum. I simply want to share this knowledge with you to *increase your awareness of your own relationship with yourself, your body and food* and to also *encourage you to transform those relationships in whatever capacity you are looking to do for yourself.*

I also wanted to create a platform where the stigma associated with the term Eating Disorders could change and rather be seen through a different lens, one in which *any and all individuals who feel they are preoccupied with food, their body and their weight more than they would like to be, can not only come together, but receive help and guidance in transforming those relationships in their lives.* This and nothing more is the goal.

In the course of this book, I will walk you through tips and tricks that will help guide you through

- Gaining awareness of ED
- Separating from ED
- Awakening your authentic self

For it is going through these three important steps that you will truly be able to fall in love with yourself, your body and your life the way you always dreamed was possible.

I truly look forward, and am honored, to be a part of this important process in your life.

Part One

The Concept of Weighing Love

The size of my pants *should* be smaller, but it isn't.
The number on my scale *shouldn't* be this number,
but it is.
The amount of calories I ate today *should* have been
less, but it wasn't.
The total number of calories I burned off today *should*
have been more, but that never happened.

A number on a scale. The size of your pants. The
amount of calories you ate today. The total number of
calories you burned off today.

Each of these numbers holds so much power, so
much influence, so much impact on your day. For
it is through these numbers that you have begun to
learn about who you are, who you should be, what you
should look like and what you shouldn't.

It is through these numbers that you have been essentially *Weighing Love* – love for yourself that is.

I know this because I have lived it. For years the number on the scale held so much power as to govern who
I viewed myself to be.

If the number was acceptable, I could continue my day feeling good. If the number was unacceptable and completely wrong, I would know that I was wrong, that I needed to change, lose weight and be skinnier.

Nowhere in these statements did I differentiate between my external body and my internal self. Somewhere along the way, the shape and size of my body overtook my entire being. The person that I was inside did not matter as much, hold as much importance or value, when my external appearance and my body was always weighing in wrong.

I share this with you to talk about something that I have learned, both professionally and personally, has extreme influential power on individuals' lives and that is the whole concept of *Weighing Love*.

The number on a scale, the size of a piece of clothing and the amount of calories consumed or burned off hold so much more than just a numeric value.

These numbers have become a means to represent who we see ourselves as.
These numbers have become a way for us to categorize ourselves as good or bad, worthy or unworthy, good enough or not good enough.

These numbers have become a means to dictate whether or not we can go to the beach, try on those shorts, buy that slice of pizza and most importantly truly love ourselves or not.

Thinking this way has led many people to become overly preoccupied with food, their bodies, their weight and their appearance.

This usually occurs automatically as a means of trying to control what is really going on in a person's life. There is a lack of what I like to call positive self-TALK.

Self-TALK is an acronym that I made up, standing for:

- *self-Trust*
- *self-Acceptance*
- *self-Love*
- *self-Knowledge*

Each of these terms holds enormous value in influencing how we view ourselves, relate to ourselves and think about ourselves daily. When we do not embody a positive self-TALK, we often turn to external means such as calorie-counting, weighing ourselves daily to have a reference point as to where we stand that day, restricting, obsessing over how many calories we burned at the gym or being attached to a certain pant size, all as a means of telling us our worth. If these numbers fit into what we perceive to be acceptable, then we can feel good about ourselves that day. But what happens, if they do not?

You may go on a diet.
You may begin to increase your cardio at the gym.
You may avoid mirrors.
You may avoid shopping.
You may begin to compare your body to others.
You may begin to compare yourself to others.
You may turn to others to bring you your happiness.
You may no longer engage in activities you enjoy because you do not feel comfortable in your own skin.
You may restrict your daily food intake.
You may begin to binge eat.
You may weigh yourself daily or even multiple times a day.
You may purge – through diet pills, diet teas, laxatives, vomiting or over-exercise.
You may call yourself fat and not good enough.
You may be hard on yourself and self-critical.
You may beat yourself up by binging or engaging in other acts of self-harm.
You may begin to see food no longer as some-

thing that is meant to nourish, but through black and white lens where everything can now be categorized as either good or bad food, right or wrong foods.

You may begin to feel bad about yourself because of these numbers.

You may begin to essentially define yourself according to these numbers.

You may view your self-worth based on these numbers.

Ultimately, you may no longer truly love yourself as a result of these numbers.

These numbers are no longer just numbers. Things that we learned in kindergarten that allow us to count, to do math and to understand how to interact with money. These numbers have now become something more, something that hold enormous power; they in turn dictate whether you are deserving of truly receiving love. Love from yourselves, love from others, and love from the world around you. You may feel that you are in loving relationships with everything I just mentioned but the truth is that unless and until you are able to see these numbers for what they are, just numbers, this is not entirely true.

As a result of feeling this way you may begin to try to control everything around you, to ensure that everything is set up right so you can attain that number which you have in mind. The number that is deemed and considered perfect. The number that you believe once reached will give you what you are truthfully looking for in all of this – permission to love yourself.

For it is self-love that we are all truly yearning for, not a number on a scale, a particular pant size or the perfect numbers consumed or burned off.

For me learning how to actually embody this notion of self-love was extremely difficult, especially because I didn't even realize that I was engaging in all of these types of behaviors as a means to attain it. I had it all backwards. For me the notion of loving myself completely could only occur when I liked the way my body looked. My body was used as a scapegoat and reasoning as to why I was not allowed to love myself. My body was the reason that I wasn't fully happy, couldn't be free to do whatever I truly wanted, couldn't choose to wear that outfit or couldn't feel confidence in who I was.

My body was the thing that needed to change, or so I thought.

Yet, the truth is it is about so much more than just having a perfect body shape. It's about loving yourself

for everything you are, everything you are not, everything you once were and everything you are working
to be.

Loving yourself comes from knowing that no matter
what happens inside of you, that whatever fears appear, you'll see them and not allow them to stop you
because you believe you are worthy of trying to create
the life of your dreams.

Learning how to fall in love with yourself is so important. I cannot believe we are never taught this alongside math and science in grade school. For when you
truly love yourself there is no greater feeling; you are
exuding that sense of love throughout your entire being, proud of who you are and what you represent.

When you have a solid love for yourself the way in
which you interact in life is a lot brighter and everything around you positively shifts. This feeling has
nothing to do with a number on a scale, the amount
of calories you burned off, the amount of calories you
ate or the size of your pants. Rather this feeling results from you truly accepting yourself for who you are
today.

As you grow to *trust, accept, love and know* yourself,
the same will begin to develop towards your body.

Because truly loving yourself also showcases itself through treating your body with the respect and love it deserves. You show this through the foods that you eat, the water you drink, the movement you allow it, the amount of rest you provide it and through having the gratitude for everything it can do for you.

> For not calling it names.
> For not cursing at it when it looks different than you think it *should* look like.
> For asking it for forgiveness when you do not treat it the way it deserves.

The notion of self-acceptance is also highly related to loving your body. For it is through firstly accepting your body for what it is today that you are on the road towards truly loving it. Yet, for so many of us this concept of self-acceptance, especially when it comes to our bodies feels utterly impossible. Instead, so many of us get focused on our weight and the size of our body to be the thing that should give us the love and happiness we are truly searching for. We begin to believe that if we can manipulate our weight, if we can change the shape of our bodies then we will be happy. We begin to only see our bodies as what they look like and how much they weigh and we overlook all the amazing things that they do for us each day.

Digestion is ignored and seen as something that our bodies should just do automatically for us.

Having legs to walk is just seen as a normal part of life and not viewed as a gift.

Breathing is something that we take for granted and we ignore the enormous power it has in keeping us alive.

From living this way, we have created a disconnection from our bodies and ultimately from ourselves. This can cause us to treat our bodies in ways it doesn't deserve.

We fail to give our body love when we choose to starve it for a day, restrict what it can eat by going on another fad diet that never works or stuffing it full of food to deal with our emotions.

We fail to listen to our body when pain arises and it is trying to tell us something is off and asking to be heard. Rather, we simply get upset and angry, as this pain is nothing but a hassle and a disruption to our day.

Our body is much wiser than we give it credit and it can only handle so much abuse, whether that be mental, emotional or physical, until it gives up and completely fights back through physical symptoms and pain.

- To truly love your body is to *know* your body and *trust* that when these symptoms come up it is your body's way of trying to communicate with you that something is unbalanced in your mental, emotional or physical life.
- To truly love your body is to listen to it when it speaks to you and to respond accordingly.
- To truly love your body is so much more than just your weight on a scale, your pant size or the shape of your buttocks. To *love* your organs, the tissues, the bones, the muscles, the fat, the hair, the skin, the blood, the plasma and the cells.
- To love your body truly means to *accept* it for what it is, what it isn't, what you wish it was and what it may be.
- To truly love yourself and your body, you must first re-establish this connection that you had with it and yourself as a young child.
- To truly love yourself and your body fully you must know that you are deserving of that.
- To truly love yourself and your body fully you must fall in love with food and see it as a gift and an ally, rather than the enemy.

- To truly love yourself and your body fully you must accept that you currently do not.
- To truly love yourself and your body fully you must believe that you can and will.

As much as I love everything I have written about in this last section of the book, in hopes of connecting and sharing with you the importance of loving yourself and your body, I do recognize that by me simply saying all of these points to you, doesn't mean that this way of thinking, acting and being, is magically going to happen overnight.

I know that what you are looking for is much more than just words. You are looking for practical steps that you can implement in your life, which in turn allows you to fall in love with yourself, your body and your life.

Because I have your best interest at heart, I decided to write the next section of this book as more of a workbook that will walk you through practical steps that you can use to help transform your relationship with yourself, your body and your life.

I am going to walk you through exercises that will take this knowledge from a place of simply recognizing that things are not exactly what you would like them to be, to a place where actual results begin to occur. These exercises are meant to allow you to look at yourself and your life in a way in which you might have never looked at it before. They are meant to enable you to understand your relationship with yourself, your body and your life in a very intimate way.

For it is the part of you that resides deep inside that we need to focus our initial attention on. By diving down into the depths of yourself, past the surface level that is filled with particular numbers and ideas of what you *should* look like, we can begin to truly address the importance of developing a positive self-TALK.

Unlike dieting which serves only as a temporary "fix", learning how to truly adopt a positive self-TALK into your everyday life results in real and lasting changes not only in all areas of your life but changes that will last for a lifetime.

This is what I want for you, not some quick and easy "solution" that never lasts. You deserve to fall in love with yourself, your body and your life – for the rest of your life!

The Importance of Building
A Positive self-TALK

Before we get into *the how to* information, you may be curious by what I exactly mean when I talk about a positive self-TALK. I believe that by acquiring these four aspects of the self a person's life will feel more fulfilled, they will obtain more happiness and feel an overall greater sense of purpose as a result of just being who they are.

- **Self-Trust:**

  Living a life upon which you truly trust yourself is highly beneficial. It will allow you to be confident in not only your choices but in areas of your life where fear or uncertainty resonates. As a result, self-doubt will no longer be able to persuade you to go in directions you do not wish to go. Being able to make decisions that are in alignment to what it is that you actually want will result in happiness.

- **Self-Acceptance:**

  We are unable to predict what our future holds for us. Therefore, we cannot chase happiness as if it will be obtained once a particular life instance takes place or we've achieved a certain weight. Living our lives this way, will not only result in us looking for happiness in all of the wrong places, but more importantly, will allow us to miss out on living in the *now*. Real happiness lies in learning how to live a life upon which you accept yourself in the present moment for everything that you are and everything that you are not. Knowing that whatever moment you are in is supposed to be occurring just as it is. Learning how to live a life like this will result in an abundance of calmness, peace and happiness to transpire.

• **Self-Love:**

Learning how to live a life upon which you authentically love the person that you are is the foundation to living the life you always dreamed was possible. The goal here is to treat yourself as you would treat your most beloved friend or family member – with an abundance of love, compassion, forgiveness, patience and understanding. Living a life where this is reflected inside each of your decisions, choices and everyday life circumstances results in authentic happiness.

- **Self-Knowledge:**

  Learning how to live a life from a place of
  knowing who you are will allow you to make
  choices and decisions that fit with what you
  actually desire. In order to know who you are
  it is essential to know what you think. What
  are your beliefs? Your desires? Your strengths?
  Your weaknesses? What are you passionate
  about? What do you have very little interest in?
  What makes you frustrated? What makes you
  blissfully happy? Knowing your conditioned
  thoughts and ED plays a big role here. They
  hold the key to uncovering the individual that
  you truly are.

You now should have a better understanding why
building and having a positive self-TALK is so important when you want to learn how to fall in love with
yourself, your body and your life. I want you to know
that if you have any questions, comments or concerns
that come up along the way, please feel free to visit my
website at www.paulagalli.com and contact me directly. I would love to help you through this process as
much as I am able.

All right, now it is time to dive right in!

Self Expression
Innocence
Self Love

August 26.1990

My bangs were short, much too short, but it didn't matter. My white seashell bathing suit showed off my pudgy tummy and little stumpy thighs, but I didn't care. My sea blue eyes instantly grabbed your attention as they were impossible to miss next to my soft ivory skin and chocolate brown hair. As I ran towards my daddy, screaming his name, all I wanted to do was swim and play. All I wanted to do was swim and play. The quiet waters of Georgian Bay were my home, were my freedom. This was where I belonged.

A true Piscean by nature you would find me nowhere else but near the water. My family often referred to me as a little fish because once I was in the water it was nearly impossible to get me out.

As I ran through the sandy shores, with my hair flowing through the wind, I didn't have a care in the world. I ran back and forth. Back and forth. With a smile on my face stretching from cheek to cheek, I would wander off on my own, as if I had been here before many times. I would fling my body into the shallow water. Duck my head in and arrive to the surface with a big grinning smile. Brushing my wet hair out of my face, I would do it again and again. I would do it again and again. I was so authentic. I was so true. I was so free. This was where I belonged.

*

I want you to think of a young child. What thoughts come to your mind? Do you envision them saying that their legs are too big, that their stomach is too flabby or that they need to lose five pounds? Do you picture this young child obsessing over the number on the scale, counting calories at meal time or comparing their diaper or short sizes with other children? Of course not! Young children exude an abundance of innocence, freedom, self-expression and self-love. They look at their reflection and see it for what it truly is, absolutely perfect. They do not curse at it, call it names or criticize it because it doesn't look the way that they have been told it should look like.

We were all children like this at some point or another. How did we get off track from this natural way of being? How did we become so disconnected from ourselves and end up no longer being able to see our reflections for what they truly are? The next section will help you begin to answer these questions.

Section A
Gaining Awareness of ED

"The unexamined life is not worth living."
- Plato

Based on what I've talked about so far, you may have realized that your relationship with yourself and your body is not necessarily coming from a place of self-love. You may have also realized that you are preoccupied with your weight, your appearance and your body more than you ever noticed or would like to be.

In order to truly transform these relationships in your life, you need to first gain awareness of who ED is and then learn about the enormous power he has in affecting your life. This section will help you do just that.

(1) Introduction to ED

The topic of the power of our minds has been popular for centuries. Aristotle, Plato, the Buddha and Albert Einstein dedicated years of their lives to learning about this one important topic. It doesn't matter which part of the planet you live on, what your customs or beliefs are, we all are influenced by our minds.

Many sayings have been developed in relation to the mind such as, "Mind over Matter" or "It's all in your head." Yet, do we even really understand what that all means?

I sure know I didn't really understand what it meant for the first twenty some years of my life. Those were just catchy sayings that didn't have that much depth or importance to me.

The power of the mind, in my opinion, lies in the fact that it has the ability to persuade us to make decisions that we might not fully one-hundred percent be behind; it has a way of urging us that we are. It has the ability to allow us to think about our greatest hopes and dreams, yet it also has the power to stop us from attaining those goals by convincing us that we can't or that we don't really care.

The power that our mind plays in affecting our lives is quite enormous. The impact that it has in influencing our behaviors, choices and the way in which we see the world is something that is really worth recognizing.

In order to be able to truly fall in love with yourself, your body and your life, learning about your thoughts is extremely important. More specifically, I believe that gaining *awareness of your thought patterns* is the first step in falling in love with yourself, your body and your life.

Without knowing what you are saying to yourself on a daily basis and the enormous power that those thoughts have in controlling and affecting your life, I feel that falling in love with yourself and your body is almost impossible.

In order to establish this awareness of your thoughts patterns, it is imperative that I introduce you to the EGO.

The EGO is something that philosophers and psychologists have discussed for decades. Different explanations for what the EGO is have been developed. However, in this book when I am speaking of the EGO I am referring to the voice that is inside of our heads.

The voice that always seems to have something to say even when you do not ask it to.
The voice that has an opinion about everything and everyone, who judges, labels and requires answers for things.
The voice that never seems to think anything is good enough, that constantly compares itself, that strives to

be something more and that always wants, needs and has to have more.

Your EGO might be saying right now, "What voice?" This response, this voice, this automatic way of thinking, is exactly what I am speaking about.

Truthfully, the EGO is the part of ourselves where most of society is currently living from. Who most of society thinks they are. Who most of society identifies themselves to be.

I decided to title this subsection, "Introduction to ED", because from my personal and professional experience, I have found that labeling the EGO, as ED, seems quite fitting. There are two reasons for this.

Firstly, within the context of this particular book the term ED can stand as the acronym for Eating Disorder. Within the introduction I explained a little bit about the Eating Disorder spectrum. I believe that if you have any negative or restricting issues with food and your body, if you over think about calories, are overly concerned about the number on the scale or anything else I spoke about in the first section of this book, then you lie somewhere on this Eating Disorder spectrum. Again, the goal is not to find where you lie on this spectrum but rather be aware that it exists. I believe that an Eating Disorder is simply just a part of one's EGO that speaks a particular language, the Eating Disorder language. I will get more into this later on.

Secondly, after living with an Eating Disorder myself, I realized that this voice in my head didn't go away after my recovery. ED may have changed his voice by no longer speaking the Eating Disorder Language, but the voice itself never disappeared. This is when I realized that this voice was actually my EGO, a voice that all human beings have inside of them.

It's a voice that strives to keep humans living from a place of fear, a place full of *shoulds* and *have tos, wants* and *needs*. A voice that tells humans that we *need* more from our lives and that we *need* to be better. A voice that on some level each one of us has inside.

As mentioned above, the only difference I have found that happens with someone who also has an Eating Disorder is that that individuals' EGO speaks a very particular language. This is what I refer to as the Eating Disorder Language. Depending on where you lie on the Eating Disorder spectrum, this language I speak of changes accordingly. However, the goal right now is not to identify whether or not you have an Eating Disorder or if you speak that language. The goal is so much bigger than that. It is to allow you to see that...

Inside of YOU, as it is inside of ALL OF US, there is an EGO.

Whether or not you feel that you have an Eating Disorder, I chose to keep the same acronym, ED, when describing the EGO, to represent what I feel each one of us has living inside of us, "Everyone's Disorder". Now you may be a bit confused and asking yourself, "What is this Paula chick talking about?! I don't have an Eating Disorder and I don't have a disorder of any kind at all!"

Before I continue, I want to be clear. When I say the word *disorder* I want to explain exactly what I mean. In our society anything with a *disorder* attached to the end of it usually has a bad rap. People often stay clear from it out of hopes of being seen in a positive light. Our society labels *disorders* as things that need to be fixed and need serious attention.

For me, I use the word *disorder* to describe exactly what it phonetically represents a *"dis-order"*. The word *dis-order* simply represents something that is out of order. On the other hand, the word *order* can be described as having things organized in a particular fashion, laid out in a row.

In this sense a *"dis-order"* would then be described as being disorganized, in a state of chaos, or disarray. The goal here is to recognize the *dis-order* that is occurring within our minds and learn techniques and tools that help clean it up. More specifically, when talking about an Eating Disorder, the goal is to recognize the *dis-order* that is occurring within your relationship and connection to eating, food and your body and correct it by having an eating *"order"*. Make sense?

I am very well aware that the definition that I have labeled ED to be, "Everyone's Disorder", may in fact trigger ED itself to react. ED may say things such as, *"What is she talking about? I don't have a disorder! There is nothing wrong with me! She is the one who had an Eating Disorder so clearly she is the one with the issues!"*

If you automatically said this or anything similar that is okay. It is quite normal. Getting on the defensive through finger pointing or being unable to see itself for what it really is very common when it comes to the EGO.

Let me be crystal clear, by no means do I think there is

something "wrong" with you. That is actually the last thing that I think. However, I do believe that gaining awareness about the powerful influence that ED has on your everyday behaviors, thoughts and actions will benefit your life. This is why I am so passionate about bringing ED's existence to you. My intention in writing this book is to provide you with tools and exercises that will allow you to fall madly in love with yourself, your body and your life.

If all of this ED labeling is confusing you, then just call it your EGO or call it Bob, call it Joe, call it Susan, call it moon, cat, car, sun, I don't care what you call it as the label doesn't really matter.

All that matters is that you realize that **you have an EGO.** Furthermore, the EGO is that part of you that is situated in fear. Yet, even though it stems from a place of fear, I don't want you to think that it is good or bad. The EGO is just what it is. The goal right now is simply to begin to acknowledge its existence, nothing more. Through beginning to develop this awareness of your EGO, you will learn that it is not you. The real you is something and someone entirely different.

As I mentioned above, most of society is living from a place where their EGO is recognized as their self. Their everyday choices, interactions and engagements are made with ED being in control. For individuals living with an ED which is an Eating Disorder, their relationship with food, their bodies, and themselves is further distorted and negatively affected.

The real you is not an Eating Disorder.

Your EGO may speak an Eating Disorder Language and you in turn may engage in disordered eating behavior, but **you are NOT an eating disorder.**

This may be difficult to understand at first, especially if ED is trying to convince you that you are. This is completely normal as ED would try to do that. ED doesn't want you to discover his existence because if you choose to break free from him he would no longer have a purpose to exist. Trust me when I tell you that this book is going to lay out all of the necessary steps which will allow you to break free from ED – both as an "Eating Disorder" and as an "Everyone's Disorder."

You may be asking yourself, why would I want to live a life without ED?

There are many reasons why you would want to distinguish yourself from ED. By doing so you will be able to live from your truth and allow the things that are holding you back from living a life you truly love living disappear.

The benefit in gaining awareness of ED is living a happier and healthier life; a life where you feel fulfilled and in connection with a bigger purpose and a sense of meaning for yourself. The truth is that ED is simply a misrepresentation of who you actually are – your authentic self.

We will get into what the authentic self is later, as for now gaining *awareness* about ED's existence is what is important.

Recap:
- The *awareness of your thought patterns* & furthermore your EGO is the first step in learning how to fall in love with yourself, your body and your life.
- The EGO = the voice that is inside of our heads that is situated in fear, which is neither good nor bad.
- Our EGOS can be labeled as ED to represent "Everyone's Disorder." For those who have an Eating Disorder, that is simply a part of their EGO that speaks a particular language, the Eating Disorder language.

(2) How to Gain Awareness of ED Through Journaling

On January 4, 1994 I received my very first diary as a Christmas present. The book had a gold lock on it with a key. I loved how the pages inside were broken up into different colored sections; pink, blue and green. Princess Jasmine and her tiger, Raja, were on the cover. Jasmine was one of my favorite Disney Princesses, besides Belle of course. Belle was always and still is my absolute favorite. My dad said I loved Belle so much as a child, that I ended up transforming into looking like her. I think it's somewhat true!

Even though this diary didn't have Belle on the cover, I still loved it. I couldn't wait to write all of my secrets inside.

From that day forward my diary became my friend, my confidante and my companion. I now had someone with whom I could share all of my secrets, thoughts, hopes, dreams and wishes. My diary would never talk back. Would never judge. Would never tell anyone what I shared with it. It would listen to what I had to say. At the young age of seven, however, I had no idea that beginning to write in that diary would help lead me to who I really was.

At the age of sixteen, I began journaling for different reasons than I had ever done before.

Rather than writing about my friends, family and the things that I was involved with, I began writing as a means to express my internal thoughts, to explore my feelings and emotions, to set intentions and goals for myself and to really begin to learn who I was.

Journaling was and still is one of the most beneficial and useful tools that has helped and still helps me check in and connect with myself on a deeper level.

In this following section I am going to talk about why I feel that you would benefit from having a journal in this process, through outlining the importance that journaling has to do with helping you fall in love with yourself, your body and your life through creating awareness of ED.

As previously mentioned, the first step in regards to having separation from ED is to gain awareness of his presence. Throughout this book I am going to be referring to ED's voice in the masculine marked by saying "his". However, you can certainly say "hers" or whatever pronoun feels comfortable for you. Gaining awareness of what ED is saying to you on a daily basis is highly important. There are certain exercises you can do in order to begin to achieve this awareness. Before I get into the exercises themselves, I suggest that you go out and buy yourself a journal as soon as you are able to.

(A)The Benefits of Journaling:

With a blank piece of paper in front of you, you are given the ability to freely express anything that you desire. Whether it is your dreams, your goals, your fears, or your insecurities, use your journal as a means to unleash anything hidden deep within. Journaling is an excellent tool to use when you are trying to make changes in your life. Though it should not serve as a replacement to talking with someone you trust, journaling is a great place for you to disclose everything that you feel inside without the thought of being judged or questioned. The best part about journaling is that there is no right or wrong way to do it. It is entirely up to you. You can choose what you want each journaling session to look like.

(B)The ABC's of Journaling:

- Affordable:

Journaling is a great self-care tool for yourself and your life. The best part is, is that all you need is a piece of paper and a pen!

- Build a Better Relationship With Yourself:

Through journaling you will begin to learn a lot more

about who you really are. Use your journal as a tool to deepen your relationship with the most important person in your life, you!

- Chitter-Chatter:

Use your journal as a place to hold all of the chitter-chatter in your mind. You will begin to feel lighter as that extra energy is no longer inside of you but rather filled throughout the pages of your journal. In turn, this will help lessen your stress levels, improve your sleep and help your overall quality of life.

(C)How to Journal:

There are many different ways to journal. Depending on what you are looking to accomplish throughout that writing session you can choose whichever journal type you desire.

You could use your journal to simply write down all of the thoughts that come to you at a particular time.

You could also use your journal to look at specific situations occurring within your life that you want to focus more on and begin to see common themes that show up for you. There is no right or wrong way to journal, the choice is entirely up to you.

(D)Tips to Help Make Your Journal Sessions More Effective:

(1) The Look/Design of the Journal:
Choose a journal that speaks to you – something that you enjoy looking at and working in. You can always buy a completely blank journal and decorate it any way you wish, to make it more personal. The important thing here is to ensure that you simply love your journal.

(2) Set the Scene:
Choose a place to journal where you feel safe to be alone with your thoughts and with doing the exercises that are going to be presented to you within this book. Some common examples are your bedroom, a park, a coffee shop or anywhere out in nature. Ensure that you are free from any distractions, such as your phone. Set the scene to have whatever makes you feel relaxed and centered. Candles, music, or a cup of warm tea are great comforting elements that will make your journal sessions more pleasurable and in turn more effective.

(3) Freedom in Your Writing:
When journaling allow yourself to write whatever comes out naturally without any source of self-editing. Make the choice to allow yourself to write whatever comes to you without placing any judgment on it.

Oftentimes there are things that want to be expressed as a means of allowing you to receive clarity towards an issue or circumstance. Remember that just because you are feeling and thinking a certain way at that particular time, it's only temporary. Allow your journal to be a safe place for you to acknowledge those passing thoughts and feelings. Allow yourself to get to a place deep within that is oftentimes hidden from your everyday reality. If you go off on tangents, great! Allow your journal sessions to lead you were they want to go.

(4) Set a Time to Journal:

It is important to plan a time to journal, as your commitment to your inner work is important in truly falling in love with yourself, your body and your life. Find a time that feels best for you. Journaling before you go to bed is a great way to let go of all of the chitter-chatter that often occurs before you go to sleep, to reflect on your thoughts and emotions and to have a different viewpoint to track your day as it is over. Others prefer to journal in the morning, or sometimes throughout the day. It really doesn't make a difference what time you journal; just choose a time that best serves you and your lifestyle. It also doesn't need to be the same time every day. The important thing is to not set rules around journaling; just commit to doing it daily.

(5)Be Consistent:
At the end of the day it doesn't matter where, how, what time or what your journal looks like, all that really matters is that you do it on a regular basis. The benefits of journaling will showcase themselves the more often you do it, I promise you that! Incorporate journaling into your daily life just like showering and brushing your teeth. Just as those serve a purpose to keep your teeth and body clean and healthy, look at journaling as a means to keep you mind and soul cleansed. The choice is yours.

(E)Different Types of Journals:
There are numerous types of journals to choose from...

My Personal Journal:
Use this journal as a place to write anything that you want at any time of the day. It could be filled with ideas, thoughts and feelings, hopes and goals, things you are thankful for, it's really up to you as there are no rules as to what your journal can be filled with.

My Dream Journal:
Keep a journal beside your bedside and write out your night's dreams every morning. You could use your dreams as a subject in a later journal entry, or if you were so inclined you could even learn how to interpret

them.

My Gratitude Journal:
Through recording what you are grateful for each day or week, such as friends, events or anything that really matters to you, you can begin to change your thought patterns to really focus on all of the blessings you have in your life.

My Ideas Journal:
This journal will be filled with all of your ideas and dreams, your visions and fantasies. These ideas can be geared towards business, family, your life, your health or anything you are inspired to work on.

My Transition Journal:
Use this journal as a means for you to focus on any transitions that you are going through such as going from high school to university, searching for a job, becoming a parent for the first time, getting married, starting a business or moving to a new city. This journal can be used to look at different patterns in your life that occur when these particular transitions are taking place.

My Travel/Vacation Journal:
While being away from the comfort of your home, new experiences occur which oftentimes bring up a lot of new feelings and emotions. Use your journal as a means of recording your time away from home and see any big differences or similarities that show up for you.

As you can see there are many types of journals that can be used in different areas of your life, depending on what you are working towards. In this particular instance I would suggest having a personal journal which you can even title, "My Journey of Breaking Free From ED" or "My Journey to Re-discovering Myself" or something that fits what it is you are wanting to accomplish from reading this book. Just make sure you are using a journal that speaks to you; the choice is totally yours. Remember there is no right or wrong when it comes to this process!

(F)Writing An Intention For Your Journaling Process
By setting a clear intention of what it is that you are wanting to achieve from writing in that particular journal you are not only allowing yourself the chance to really dig deep to uncover what it is that you really desire, but furthermore, you are proclaiming to the

universe that this is what you would like to bring into your life. Simply focus your mind on what it is that you would like to accomplish for yourself and your life throughout this journaling process. In this section you could incorporate the following statement,

"By the time I finish writing in this journal and there are no pages left I ....."

Think of this statement as something to help you get clear on what you would like to accomplish by the end of that journal.

Again, remember there is no right or wrong. Anything you would like to accomplish is wonderful and possible!

Here are just some examples of things you could write:

By the time I finish writing in this journal and there are no pages left I...

> I am kind to myself.
> I have freedom with food.
> I told somebody about what I am going through.
> I accept myself.

I love myself.
I treat my body kindly.
I accept my body.
I love my body.
I have a positive relationship with food.
I look at food with love.
I eat a full meal with my family.
I go shopping for new pants.

Notice that the above examples are written out in present tense. In the next section I will explain why this is important.

You can begin to fill in the rest of this statement by answering the following questions.

Why did you pick up this book to begin with? What were you hoping to achieve? What did you need help with? What is missing from your life that is causing you not to be in love with yourself, your body, food and your life?

_____

_____

_____

_____

_____

_____

_____

_____

Through completing this first exercise, you are beginning to challenge ED's voice. By this, I mean that oftentimes ED tries to convince us that what we really wish we could accomplish is impossible.

When you think about what you really want, what thoughts instantly come up? What are those thoughts saying? By listening to what thoughts are occurring within your mind you can begin to hear ED's voice. He may be saying things like, *"What I really would like to accomplish isn't possible"* or *"You can't accomplish anything by the end of this journal. It's one book, what's really going to change by the end of it?"*

Maybe he isn't saying those exact words but he may be trying to convince you of something that is out of alignment with what you truly want for yourself and your life. Again, I want to remind you that this voice is ED – not the real you. In spite of what ED may be saying to you, no matter how loud or mean he may get, I want to encourage you to find the strength you had when you decided to pick up this book and please write down what you want, even if it feels impossible or silly.

Something to recognize in this exercise is that you ***do not need to know how*** you will accomplish what you want. What you ***do need to have is the belief*** that change can and will take place in your life.

Your job here is to simply tell ED to be quiet for a minute and write down what you wish could be accomplished if it could be guaranteed that it was possible. If you were unable to really get clear of what you wanted from answering the questions, you may be able to find out this answer by finishing the following statement...

If anything were possible, by the time I finished writing in this book I....

_____

_____

_____

_____

_____

_____

_____

_____

_____

_____

_____

_____

_____

_____

_____

_____

_____

_____

_____

_____

_____

_____

_____

_____

_____

Remember when doing this exercise you do not need to know "the how", you simply need to **believe** that on some level what you want to accomplish is possible. Through stating what you hope to achieve you in turn can set an intention for it.

(G)Intentions are Written In First Person, Present Tense & Positive Mode

When writing this intention it is important to write it in first person, present tense and in the positive form.

By this I mean if you would like to have a greater relationship with yourself, you wouldn't write *"I will have a better relationship with myself."* Rather you would write, *"I have a better relationship with myself."*

If you were to write something such as, *"I will no longer put myself and my life second on the list of my priorities."* I encourage you to write it in the positive and present tense such as, *"I am putting myself and my life first on my list of priorities."*

This is extremely important because you are beginning to train your mind to think differently, which in turn will allow your life to be different, even if it doesn't feel right or truthful at that very moment.

It is important to note the reasoning why writing in this particular context is so important. For example, if you were to write this statement in the future tense such as, *"I will be kind to myself"*, you are always living in the someday, one day mentality. In this sense it will always be a goal in the future and will never occur, as you are somewhat waiting for it to happen one day. That is not what we want. We want to start using techniques and tools that are going to allow your life to change today.

I would like you to close your eyes, take a deep breath, allow ED's questions, fears and doubts to quiet and ask yourself what you really are intending to achieve from committing to reading and working through the exercises in this next section of the book. With that clear intention fresh in your mind, I would like you to write it onto the first page of your journal. You can title this page something like, "My Intention For This Journal" or "My Intention In Writing In This Journal".

Now that your journal is all set up and ready to go, it is time to get back to what we initially were talking about; gaining awareness of ED. Through the intention exercise you may have just been able to hear ED's voice. If you were not able to hear it, no worries! The following exercises will also allow you the opportunity to become aware of ED's existence.

(3) Exercises Towards Gaining Awareness of ED

Gaining awareness of ED is the first step in truly falling in love with yourself, your body and your life. Below you will find a list of questions for you to answer in your journal.

It is very important for you to answer all of the questions in each section at the same time. You can, however, take breaks between answering each section of questions.

If you are anything like I was at the age of sixteen, I know that going inside of yourself and answering these types of questions may seem a bit strange and foreign to you. Please don't try to figure out what these questions have to do with ED, as that is not the intention of this exercise. Right now all you need to think about is taking your time and answering these questions as honestly as possible, as there are no right or wrong answers.

I promise you that the more you answer these types of questions the easier they will become.

Lastly, these responses are for your eyes only, unless you choose to share them with others, so there is no need to worry about what others may think. Remember, this is your journey, no one else's.

1. **<u>Your Internal Qualities-</u>**
- How would you describe yourself? What type of person are you?
- How do you think others would describe you?
- Do you think you are smart? Why or why not?
- Do you think you are funny? Why or why not?
- Do you think you are a nice person? Why or why not?
- List FIVE qualities you like about yourself. Why do you like these things?
- List FIVE qualities you do not like about yourself. Why do you not like these things?

- How do you feel about yourself when you are alone?
- How do you feel about yourself when you are in public?
- Would you say you're your own best friend? Why or why not?
- Would you say you are hard on yourself? Why or why not?
- Do you think you expect a lot from yourself? Why or why not?
- Do you feel that you should always be striving for more? Why or why not?
- Do you ever feel the need to be viewed as perfect or the best at everything? Why or why not?
- Do you compare your internal qualities to others? Why or why not?
- If so what do you usually think when you are comparing your internal qualities to others?

2. **Your Appearance-**
- Do you think you are pretty? Why or why not?
- What parts of your appearance do you like?
- Why do you like them?
- What part of your appearance do you wish were different?
- Why do you wish they were different?
- How do you feel about your appearance when you are alone?

- How do you feel about your appearance when you are in public?
- If your appearance could look anyway you wanted what would it look like?
- Why would it look like this?
- Do you compare your appearance to others? Why or why not?
- If so what do you usually think when you are comparing your appearance to others?
- How do you think you would feel if your appearance looked the way you wished it could?
- Has the way you view your appearance stopped you from doing something you really wanted to do? If so please explain that experience(s).

3. **Your Body-**
- What parts of your body do you like?
- Why do you like them?
- What part of your body do you wish were different?
- Why do you wish they were different?
- How do you feel about your body when you are alone?
- How do you feel about your body when you are in public?
- If your body could look anyway you wanted what would it look like?
- Why would it look like this?

- Do you compare your body to others? Why or why not?
- If so what do you usually think when you are comparing your body to others?
- How do you think you would feel if your body looked the way you wished it could?
- Has the way you view your body stopped you from doing something you really wanted to do? If so please explain that experience(s).

4. **<u>Your Weight-</u>**
- Are you happy with how much you weigh?
- Do you think you should gain weight? Why or why not?
- Do you think you should lose weight? Why or why not?
- Do you compare your weight to others weight? Why or why not?
- If so what do you usually think when you are comparing your weight to others?
- Has your weight ever stopped you from doing something you really wanted to do? If so please explain that experience(s).

5. **<u>The Scale-</u>**
- Do you own a scale? Why or why not?
- How often to you weigh yourself?
- What are you *thinking* before you step on the

scale?
- What are you *thinking* when you step on the scale and see your weight?
- What are you *thinking* after you step off the scale?
- How do you *feel* about yourself before you get on the scale?
- How do you *feel* about yourself when you are on the scale and see your weight?
- How do you *feel* about yourself when you step off the scale?

6. **Food/Dieting-**
- How would you describe your relationship with food?
- What types of foods do you normally tend to eat?
- What types of foods do you normally crave?
- What types of foods do you normally try to stay away from?
- Are you afraid of eating any certain food groups? (i.e. fats, proteins, carbs) If so, which ones and why?
- Are you afraid of eating any particular foods? If yes, please write down the list of your fear foods and explain why you are afraid of them.
- Do you feel that food holds any power over you? Explain why or why not.

- Do you prefer to eat alone? Why or why not?
- What are your thoughts and opinions in regards to eating in public?
- Have you ever skipped a meal on purpose? If so, please explain why?
- Have you ever hidden food? If so, what did you hide, where did you hide it and why did you hide it?
- Have you ever binged? If so, what did you binge, where did you binge and what time did you binge? Do you have any idea around why you binge?
- Do you count calories? Why or why not? If you do, how long have you been counting them for? What are you hoping to achieve by counting calories?
- Have you ever not eaten something because of its caloric content? If so please explain why.
- Have you ever dieted? Why did you?
- Have you ever taken diet pills? If so why and how many times?
- Have you ever taken laxatives? If so why and how many times?
- Have your ever purged? If so how often and why do you think you purged?

7. **<u>Restaurants-</u>**
- Do you have any issues eating at a restaurant?

Why or why not?
- When you think about going to a restaurant what comes up for you? (i.e. *thoughts* and *feelings*)
- When you are in a particular restaurant what is going through your mind when you are looking at the menu?
- When the food comes to the table for yourself and your company what goes through your mind?
- Have you ever not gone out with friends or family because of the restaurant choice others made? If so please explain why.
- Have you ever eaten alone at a restaurant? Why or why not?
- Would you ever eat alone at a restaurant? Why or why not?

8. <u>Bathing Suit-</u>
- When you have to put on a bathing suit what comes up for you? (i.e. *thoughts* and *feelings*)
- Do you like being in public when you are in a bathing suit? Why or why not?
- Do you like being alone when you are in a bathing suit? Why or why not?
- Has needing to be in a bathing suit ever stopped you from doing something you really wanted to do? If so please explain that

experience(s).

9. **Comparison to Others-**
- What do you *think* when you see someone who you think is pretty?
- What do you *think* when you see someone who has a body you like?
- How do you *feel* about yourself when you see someone who you think is pretty?
- How do you *feel* about yourself when you see someone who has a body you like?
- What do you *think* when you see models? Girls on the cover of magazines? Movie stars?
- How do you *feel* about yourself when you see models? Girls on the cover of magazines? Movie stars?
- Has the way others looked ever stopped you from doing something you really wanted to do? If so, please explain that experience(s).

10. **Exercise/Being Active-**
- What is your opinion of working out, being active and exercise?
- Do you currently work out? Why or why not?
- If you do not work out do you want to? What's stopping you from being active today?
- If you do work out and/or are active please answer the following questions...

- What type of exercise do you do?
- How many times a week do you work out?
- Do you go to the gym? Why or why not?
- Do you focus on calories when you are at the gym or in any work out?
- What is your main intention for working out

Recap:
- On a scale of 1-10, where 1 is very easy and 10 is very difficult, how would you rate your experience of answering all of those questions above?
- What was the easiest part in answering all of the above questions?
- What was the most difficult part in answering all of the above questions?
- Did you learn anything about yourself that you didn't know before you answered these questions?
- If so, please describe what you learned.
- What was the most surprising thing that you learned about yourself from answering these questions?

I AM AWESOME EXERCISE!

Before we continue I want to acknowledge you and tell you that you should be really proud of yourself. You just answered a lot of questions about yourself and your life.

What I am about to tell you to do next may feel unnatural or a bit strange, but I would like you to take a moment and acknowledge all of the great work you have already done so far.

Even if it feels weird, I want you to now tell yourself, "I am awesome!"

Say it once more and really believe it! Seriously, as awkward as it sounds, just do it!

Okay, now that you remember how awesome you are, let's continue.

(4) Where Do Most of ED's Opinions and Beliefs Come From?

Keeping your awareness exercises from above in mind, where do you think most of these answers came from? More specifically, where do you think most of ED's opinions and beliefs came from?

Your answers may include some or all of following:
- your family
- your friendships
- your culture
- your community
- your generation
- the society you live in
- the media

If you think of a young child being born as a clean slate and it is through their interactions with their family, their community and society at large that they learn certain social cues like what is right or wrong. Many of ED's opinions develop unconsciously from those influences. By no means am I saying that everything you learned while you were growing up is bad or didn't have a good overall purpose in trying to set boundaries, guidelines and structures for you to follow. However, oftentimes as we get older if we never take a step back and re-evaluate what our current beliefs and views are, we can find that we are auto-matically continuing to engage in behaviors that do not necessarily serve our highest interest and, further-more, reflect who we really are or who we really want to be.

I remember when I started thinking about my life from this perspective. It felt very foreign and strange. Up until that point, I had spent my entire life living the way I thought I was supposed to be living. Being the person I thought I was supposed to be.

This all took place unconsciously of course. Rather than being curious about anything that I was taught, I just assumed it was correct. I did not have the un-derstanding or awareness to even think about ques-tioning my opinions, viewpoints, thoughts or beliefs. Rather than wondering if what I was thinking was true or not, I automatically identified with and was attached to my thoughts as a representation of who I believed I was. Living in this unconscious state is quite common because ED's opinions and viewpoints have become so engrained in us that we truly believe they are our own.

It is important to note that these same types of uncon-scious cues that were taught to us can directly affect and influence the way in which you view your body, food, eating, your weight and how you see yourself overall. I know it certainly did for me. We will get more into this later on.

As for now, as you work through the next section, you will begin to uncover more information about yourself and your life. Remember, it is through *awareness* that any real and lasting change can take place. Without that kind of self-knowledge and awareness, it is almost impossible for things to truly shift.

(5) Exercises Around ED's Influences On His Opinions and Beliefs

Using your journal, answer the following questions as honestly as possible. Just like with the last exercise, it is not necessary for you to answer all of these questions at once but it is important for you to answer all of the questions in each section at the same time.

Again, please don't try to second guess and try to figure out what these questions have to do with ED before you answer them. That is not the intention of this exercise. Right now all you need to think about is taking your time and answering these questions as honestly as possible.

Remember, this is your journey, no one else's. These

responses are for your eyes only, unless you choose to share them with others, so there is no need to worry about what others may think of your responses.

1) **How Your Family has Played a Role in Influencing Your Opinions and Beliefs**
- Is family an important part of your life? Why or why not?
- Do you think family is an important part of life for the other members of your family? Why or why not?
- Do you/did you ever eat dinner with your family or do family things together?
- What would you say is the thing you love most about your family?
- What would you say is the thing you love least about your family?
- Are both your parents alive? If not what does your current home dynamic look like?
- Do you live with your parents?
- Are your parents married or separated?
- If married, please describe your perception of the type of relationship they have.
- If separated, please explain when this happened and how that experience affected you? Are you happier or sadder that they are no longer together? Why?
- Do you have any siblings? If so, are you older?

younger? or in the middle of them?

- What is the relationship you have with your siblings?
- What is the relationship that you have with your parents?
- What would you say are some of your family's expectations of how you should be?
- How would you say your family interacts with one another?
- How many hours a week would you say you spend with any of your family members?
- What is the financial status of your family?
- Would you consider your family as being lower class, middle class or upper class?
- How would you say that your family's financial status has influenced your life?
- Which of these statements most accurately describes your family?
  - My family says things like, "I love you" and we hug one another but I do not feel emotionally connected to them
  - My family tends to stay on the surface, i.e. we talk about surface things such as business, the news, fashion, music and so on but never touch upon feelings or emotions.
  - My family and I are very open emotion-ally, i.e. we always talk about what is go-

ing on in our lives, as well as our feelings
and emotions
- o My family is always in conflict. There
  always seems to be yelling, fighting and
  problems going on. These problems are
  never dealt with but rather brushed and
  pushed aside.
- o My family is not like any of these above
  examples.
- o My family is a combination of these
  above examples. If so which ones?
- Regardless of which answer you most related
  to from the six examples above, please describe
  what your family dynamic is like in as much detail as you can. What are the general patterns
  of how you relate to each other?
- What is your families' opinion about weight?
  Physical appearance? Food?
- If you could change anything about your family
  what would it be?
- What would your dream family life be like?
- How would you describe that your family has
  influenced your opinion of your looks? Your
  body? Your weight? Yourself as a person? Your
  relationship with food?

2) How Your Friendships Have Played a Role in Influencing Your Opinions and Beliefs

- Are friendships an important part of your life? Why or why not?
- Describe the dynamic you have with your current friendships? How did you meet? How long have you known one another? What do you usually do together?
- What would you say is the thing you love most about your friends?
- What would you say is the thing you love least about your friends?
- How do you and your friends interact with one another?
- How many hours a week would you say you spend with your friends?
- How would you describe your friends out of the following:
  - My friends and I say things like, "I love you" and we hug one another but I do not feel emotionally connected to them
  - My friendships usually tend to stay on the surface, i.e. we talk about surface things such as business, the news, fashion, music and so on but never touch upon feelings or emotions.
  - My friends and I are very open emotion-

ally, i.e. we always talk about what is going on in our lives, as well as our feelings and emotions

- o My friendships always seem to be in conflict or are filled with drama, i.e. there always seems to be yelling, fighting and problems going on. These problems are never dealt with but rather brushed and pushed aside.
- o My friendships are not like any of these above examples.
- o My friendships are a combination of these above examples. If so, which ones?

- Regardless of which answer you most related to from the six examples above, please describe what your friendships are like in as much detail as you can. How do you interact with your circle of friends?
- What are you friends' opinions about weight? Physical appearance? Food?
- How would you describe that your friends have influenced your opinion of your looks? Your body? Your weight? Yourself as a person? Your relationship with food?

3) How Your Culture has Played a Role in Influencing Your Opinions and Beliefs

- What type of background/culture does your family come from?
- Describe where you were born.
- Describe where your parents were born.
- Did you grow up in the same cultural environment as your parents? As your grandparents? As your sibling(s)?
- What are some of your cultural customs? Traditions? Ways of life?
- What is your culture's opinion on the dynamics of relationships? i.e. Marriages, Siblings, Friendships, Family
- What is your culture's opinion of sharing their emotions?
- What are some of your culture's expectations of how men should be?
- What are some of your culture's expectations of how women should be?
- What are some of your culture's expectations of education? Work? Family Life?
- What is your cultures' opinion about weight? Physical appearance? Food?
- How would you describe that your culture has influenced your opinion of your looks? Your body? Your weight? Yourself as a person? Your relationship with food?

4) **How Your Community has Played a Role in Influencing Your Opinions and Beliefs**

- How would you describe the community that you were born in?
- If you have lived in different communities throughout your life, how would you describe those communities?
- Did you grow up in the same community as your parents? As your sibling? As your grandparents?
- What are some of your community's expectations of how men should be?
- What are some of your community's expectations of how women should be?
- What are some of your community's expectations of education? Work? Family Life?
- What is your community's' opinion about weight? Physical appearance? Food?
- How would you describe that your community has influenced your opinion of your looks? Your body? Your weight? Yourself as a person? Your relationship with food?

5) **How The Society You Live In has Played a Role in Influencing Your Opinions and Beliefs**

- Were you born in the Western hemisphere? If so where? If not, where were you born?
- Were your parents born in the Western hemisphere? If so where? If not where were they born?
- Have you ever visited other parts of the world other than where you were born? If so, please state the places you have visited and give a description of your experience within these places.
- Have you ever visited a developing country? If so, please state the places you have visited and give a description of your experience within these countries.
- How has the society that you have lived in influenced your life?
- What are some of the expectations of how men should be within the society you live in/grew up in?
- What are some of the expectations of how women should be within the society you live in/ grew up in?
- What are some of the expectations of how education is viewed and valued within the society you live in/grew up in?

- Work Life? Family Life?
- What is your society's opinion about weight? Physical appearance? Food?
- How would you describe that your society has influenced your opinion of your looks? Your body? Your weight? Yourself as a person? Your relationship with food?

6) **How Your Generation has Played a Role in Influencing Your Opinions and Beliefs**
- What year were you born in?
- What were some of the most popular things, such as games, musical influences, technological devices, gadgets, and so on that were around when you were a child? A teenager? A young adult?
- What would you say are the major differences between your generation and your parent's generation?
- What is your generation's opinion about weight? Physical appearance? Food?
- How would you describe that your generation has influenced your opinion of your looks? Your body? Your weight? Yourself as a person? Your relationship with food?

7) How The Media has Played a Role in Influencing Your Opinions and Beliefs

- How would you describe your relationship with the media? Do you watch shows about celebrities and entertainment news? Read different pop magazines?
- Do you find that you are easily influenced by what you see on TV? Read in magazines? See in pictures?
- Describe what you believe is the media's standard for beauty.
- Do you agree with this standard? Why or why not?
- Describe what you believe is the media's standard for an acceptable body type.
- Do you agree with this standard? Why or why not?
- Describe the media's influence on music.
- What type of music do you like?
- Do you feel that the type of music that you are into is highly connected and influenced by the media?
- What types of images and ideas do mainstream media promote as being normal and acceptable?
- What types of images and ideas do mainstream media promote as not being normal and acceptable?

- How would you describe that the media has influenced your opinion of your looks? Your body? Your weight? Yourself as a person? Your relationship with food?

Recap:
- On a scale of 1-10, where 1 is very easy and 10 is very difficult, how would you rate your experience of answering all of those questions above?
- What was the easiest part in answering all of the above questions?
- What was the most difficult part in answering all of the above questions?
- Did you learn anything about yourself that you didn't know before you answered these questions?
- If so please describe what you learned.
- What was the most surprising thing that you learned about yourself from answering those following questions?

I AM AWESOME EXERCISE!

Just as with the last exercise, before we continue I want to acknowledge you and tell you that you should be really proud of yourself. You just answered a lot of questions about your life. In order to answer all of these questions it really takes a person who is strong, determined and willing to do what it takes to better their life. I know you are that person and if you don't know that about yourself yet, hopefully you are beginning to see the fire that you have inside of you to do what it takes to achieve a better life.

Remember, if you *want* it you will achieve it. You do not need to know *how* all you need to do is *believe* it is possible.

I would like you to take this moment to acknowledge yourself on all of the great work you just did again.

Now tell yourself, "I am awesome!" Say it twice more and really believe it!

Now that you've reminded yourself of how awesome you are, let's continue in gaining awareness of ED.

(6) How Did These Influences Affect ED's Opinion?

You may be wondering why I asked you to answer so many questions about yourself and your life.

Answering these types of questions is one of the most important steps you can take in breaking free from ED, because it allows you to gain conscious awareness of some of your current opinions and beliefs.

It also may allow you to see how your opinions and beliefs may have been formulated and possibly influenced you to think or see things in a certain way. Breaking free from ED will first begin to happen when you are aware of how his thought patterns have affected your opinions about yourself, your body and your life.

Again, without this level of conscious awareness of what he thinks, breaking free from ED and living a life you truly wish you were living is a lot harder, if not impossible. Right now, you may completely believe that all of your current thoughts and opinions make up who you truly are. I am not saying that you are wrong or right. However, all I ask from you is to keep an open mind when I say that may not be entirely true.

You may be asking yourself how I was able to realize that ED's thoughts and influences were a story and not really me. That's a great question!

I know from personal experience that I had a very difficult time believing the things I've been talking about so far when I first set out to change my life. Until my early twenties, I was walking around the world being a particular version of Paula that I was so convinced that I was. What I didn't know during this time was that ED had actually created a story around who I associated "this Paula" to be.

Just like how an MP3 player only plays whatever songs were uploaded to it, my mind automatically told me the story that ED made up about who "this Paula" was. This story played within my mind daily and as a result dictated a lot of my choices, behaviors and actions. This story was happening unconsciously of course and I had no idea that it was playing such a role in affecting my opinion about myself, about my body, about food, about my weight, about others and about my life in general. Truth be told, the story that ED was telling me daily, was just a part of my EGO, something I didn't even realize existed at that time

The story that ED had been telling me about myself

began from the young age of nine. My desire to lose weight was always about covering something else that was hidden much deeper inside. A lack of self-esteem. A lack of identity. A need to be accepted. This desire to lose weight was directly related to the same old story that I had been saying to myself for years. A story that did not feel like a *story* at all, but rather the person I saw myself as for over a decade of my life.

You may be asking yourself, well where did this story come from? If we were all born as free beings, with an abundance of self-love how did Paula's story become so distorted? The following section showcases a glimpse into some of my past experiences, which may help explain how the story of "this Paula" was created.

*

GRADE FOUR
September 12.1995
Dear Diary,
Today I went to Katie's house to play with her. She told me a secret that she said not to tell anyone so the secret was yesterday I wore a bra to school. So Katie heard that Michael said that I have big boobs to Matt but it's not my fault, if I had a choice I would not want to get them till I'm older.

October 16.1995

As I stared at my reflection in the mirror, I was completely unable to recognize what I saw. This was not the same girl who stood here months, even weeks, before. I was wearing a light green, beige and pink training bra with flowers all over it. I didn't like the fact that I had to wear a bra, but I had breasts now, so I had to. *What happened to my body? Why did so many things change? Why do I have such big boobs all of a sudden? Why are my thighs so big? Why are my hips so wide? Why do I have extra hair all over?* As I tightly grabbed hold of my breasts and thighs, I closed my eyes and prayed to God to take all of this extra stuff off of my body. I opened my eyes to see that nothing had changed. I stared at my body. Up and down. Up and down.

None of this made sense to me. None of my friends at school or dance class looked like this. *Why do I look like this? Maybe this was all just a bad dream. When I wake up tomorrow morning, everything will be back to normal, it just has to be.* So I went to bed that night certain that in the morning I would look like my old self again. Beep! Beep! As I reached over to turn my alarm off, I remembered what I prayed for before falling asleep last night. I instantly jumped out of bed, more excited than I did on Christmas morning and ran to the mirror, fully knowing that my prayers would have been answered. Tears began streaming down my face. Nothing had changed at all. Without saying a word at all I screamed at my reflection, which I was so closely staring at. *Why is this happening to me!?! I hate my body! I'm so disgusting! My boobs are so big. My thighs are so thick. My hips are so wide. There is something wrong with me. I am not normal. I am not normal.*

*

Nothing had physically disappeared that morning, like I had asked for, but something much more important vanished instead. My body was four years older than my mind. The two did not link up causing confusion. Causing distress. Causing insecurities. Causing self-doubt. I was still a little girl who wanted to play with my friends and Barbie dolls, yet my body spoke differently.

I was still a little girl who wanted to be Belle from *Beauty and the Beast*, yet, my body looked as if I was a teenager, and a teenager surely wasn't who I was. My new body had completely eliminated my confidence in who I was and my ability to simply be a child. From this day forward, my childhood days were gone. I looked like I was 13 years old and as a result people treated me as if I was this age. Four years of my childhood were about to vanish, yet I had no idea.

I no longer had any positive connection to my own reflection. All I saw was this unfamiliar figure staring back at me in my perfect pink and purple bedroom. From that day forward I labeled myself as different and being different at nine years old was the last thing that I wanted. I didn't want to be different than any of my friends. Than anyone else. Being different was bad. Being different made me stand out. Being different meant that there was something wrong with me. Something abnormal with me. Something that needed to be fixed.

Feeling different automatically resulted in me disconnecting from the young girl that I really was. I was now trapped. Trapped inside of my mind. My mind, which was filled with insecurities, self-doubt, uneasiness, worries, anxiety and fear. My mind that was filled with fictitious stories that I was truly beginning to believe were true. In my mind I was no long normal. I was irregular. Abnormal. Nonstandard. Atypical. Unusual. Odd. Malformed. Strange. I was anything but normal and normal was all I wanted to be.

*

GRADE FIVE
August 30.1997
I was sitting behind my bedroom door talking to a group of boys on the phone. I was extremely excited,

yet completely nervous at the same time. This was the first group of guys that I had really spoken to who didn't go to my school. The topic of conversation suddenly turned to the size of my breasts. "Your boobs are bigger than my moms," one of the boys said. I froze and listened to all of them laughing at me on the other end. I laughed back, trying to act like it didn't bother me, but it did. I didn't like being laughed at. I hung up the phone. Tears began to fill my eyes. I turned to my left and was face to face with myself in the mirror. *What's wrong with me? See I am such a freak. No one else I know has boobs the size of people's parents. I hate my body. I hate my body. I hate it. I wish I was normal.* Tears continued streaming down my face. *I wish I was perfect.*

*

I didn't know who I was. I didn't have any idea. So I turned to those around me to show me. My sister. My friends. The media. The Spice Girls. I constantly compared myself to others. My eyes to their eyes. My legs to their legs. My breasts to their breasts. I was always attracted to anything and everything that was much different than my own appearance. Blonde hair. Long legs. Tanned skin. Thick hair. Small breasts. I constantly wanted to be someone else. Something else. Something that I was convinced was right. Perfect. Was the way that I had to be in order to survive – more importantly, in order to become happy. To become perfect. For almost two years now I had been thinking this way. To me constantly comparing, constantly wanting to be anything other than me was completely normal to me. This was just how I had to be.

*

GRADE SIX
August 18.1998
I stood in my perfect pink and purple room. Staring at myself much more deeply than I had ever done before. I thought of how I felt when I was performing my dance routine last week. *I am not skinny enough to be a dancer. I am too curvy. I am too fat.* My eyes became fixated on my breasts. *My boobs are so big. Ahhh I hate them. I am so sick of being the only one who has to wear a sport bra in class. I hate that the boys all make comments about my breasts.* I stared at my thighs. *I am so fat. I hate that I look like this. I hate my body. I just want to be the same as everyone else. Like all of my friends. Like my sister. Like Posh Spice.* I turned and looked at the Spice Girls posters that I had hanging on my wall. I stared at Victoria. Then looked back at myself in the mirror. *Why am I so much chubbier than she is? I want to look like her. I want to be just as skinny as she is. If I looked like her then I would be happy. I just know it. I need everything to shrink. I need everything to get smaller.*

*I need it to. I just need it to. If I lose weight, then my
curves will get smaller. That's what I am going to do.
I am just going to lose weight, I have to. I just have
to. Once I lose weight then everything will be better. I
wish I was perfect. I wish I was perfect.*

*

REALITY. What is actually occurring. The present
moment. No stories attached. No hidden meanings.
No assumptions added. Reality was that I was different than everyone else. I was taller. More developed. I
did stand out. That wasn't in my head. That was reality.

Yet, I didn't have the slightest idea of how to accept
the reality that was my body. I was unsure of how to
accept the reality that was my life. I didn't enjoy it; actually I hated it. I didn't know how to be myself inside
of this new body. I didn't know who I was so I escaped
reality. My mind created an alternative world which I
was living inside of. It was filled with all of my biggest
insecurities and only helped me continue living in that
way. Through living my life like this I was no longer
living in the present moment, in the reality of the day.

This is when baby ED was born, yet I had no idea.

*

GRADE SEVEN
September 30.1998
I grabbed my little white book with bright pink hearts all over it and opened it up to the first page. *Okay, so it is almost the day. I am going to lose all of my weight, my curves will shrink and then I will look like everyone else. Time to enter all of the important information. Current weight. 107. God I remember when I weighed like 80 pounds. I am so fat now. I want to be less than 100 pounds. 100 pounds means I am fat. So that means I need to lose like at least 15 pounds. Right. Yeah 15 pounds sounds perfect. I bet my curves will shrink a lot if I get to that size. What else do I need to enter? Umm, I guess tomorrow's date. I am starting at the beginning of the new month. That makes the most sense. I think that is how you are supposed to start dieting right? At the beginning of the week. Or the beginning of the month. I will start at the beginning of the month, since that is tomorrow. So after I do this and lose all this weight, I will look like everyone else. My body will be like all the other girls in my dance class. Be like my sister. Be like my friends. Be like Posh Spice. Skinny. Yeah I can't wait until I will look perfect.*

October 1.1998
Diet Day One: Breakfast
So today is the first day of my diet. That means I am

not allowed to eat any junk food because junk food is bad. I should also not eat a lot because that will make me fatter. So what am I going to have for breakfast? I guess I will have cereal and milk. Yeah that's healthy. For lunch I will have whatever my mom packs me. She never really gives me junk anyways. Sometimes I wish she would. But now I don't so I guess that's good.

Diet Day One: Lunch
I hate this sandwich. It's so boring. All my friends have cool lunches. Like dunk-a-roos or lunchables. But I guess I shouldn't eat that stuff anyways. Not if I want to lose weight. I guess I will just eat what my mom made for me.

Diet Day One: Dinner
So we are having pasta and salad for dinner. Pasta is bad for you I think but I don't know why. I don't really know. But what else am I going to eat? I have to eat pasta because it's all my parents are making for me. Whatever I am sure it's fine. At least I am having salad too.

Diet Day One: Late Night
Can't have any dessert tonight. Not if I want to lose weight. Dessert is bad. Desert is not good. Can't have any dessert tonight. Dessert will make me fat.

October 2.1998
Diet Day Two: Breakfast
Okay so I guess I will have cereal and milk again for breakfast. That's healthy.

Diet Day Two: Lunch
Same old lunch. Carrots and celery as a snack and an apple. This is all good food. Yeah, if I keep eating like this I am going to lose weight in no time.

Diet Day Two: Dinner
We are having chicken parmesan tonight. I love chicken parmesan! We are also having green beans and potatoes. This is all healthy. Good.

Diet Day Two: Late Night
My sister is having ice cream. Why can't I have any? Why is she skinner than me and able to eat ice cream and I am not? This isn't fair. This isn't fair at all. I want ice cream too. No, I can't I need to stick to my diet. I need to not eat bad food and ice cream is bad.

October 3.1998
Diet Day Three: Breakfast
Okay, so I am sick of eating cereal. I will have a slice of toast instead. A slice of toast and peanut butter. Peanut butter is healthy, it has peanuts.

Diet Day Three: Lunch

It's Friday that means I am having tuna. Every Friday I have tuna, because I am Catholic and Catholic people don't eat meat on Fridays. I still don't understand why tuna isn't considered a meat, but my mom said it isn't. So tuna is healthy. Carrots and celery too. My mom packed me a cookie today but I can't eat it. Cookies are bad. Cookies will make me get fat. I gave my cookie away to a friend in my class.

Diet Day Three: Dinner

We are having more fish tonight for dinner. We are also having rice and broccoli. This is all healthy. This is all good food. This is a good dinner.

Diet Day Three: Night

Oh no it's Friday night. That means it's chips night. We are only allowed to eat chips once a week and it's always on Fridays. Daddy makes popcorn and then we have popcorn and chips. We get to drink pop too. And we watch TGIF. I love TGIF. It has the best shows. Well I want to eat the chips. I have been good for almost three days. I will just eat the chips and popcorn tonight. I want to. I want to. I am going to eat them everyone else is. I guess I am not dieting anymore. Whatever. It wasn't even working anyways my body still looks the same.

In grade seven I started getting more attention from boys in comparison to the few years prior. The only boy that I felt ever paid attention to me who I liked back was this guy I liked since grade two, but that had been a long time ago and he no longer went to my school anyways. There was a new boy who just came to my school and he wanted to be my boyfriend. I remember feeling so excited about this. He was the first guy that actually wanted to be my boyfriend. A week or so later I found out he only liked me because of my boobs. My self-esteem lowered. I was angry and broke up with him right away. *Why can't anyone like me for me? Why do they only like me because of my boobs? Boys only like me because I have big boobs.*

*

July 27.1999
One of my best friends, Kyla called me on the phone; she was all excited and asked me what I was doing that weekend. I don't know. Let's go to my cottage!!!! *I don't want anyone to see me in a bathing suit.* Yeah I don't know if I can go. Why not? Why can't you go? *Because I don't want anyone to see me in a bathing suit.* Well, I have to check with my parents. *And even if they say yes, I don't want to go. I don't want anyone to see me in a bathing suit.* Okay yeah check with

them and let me know. It will be so fun if you come. We will hang out on the beach. *Yeah I know that and I don't want to be seen in a bathing suit. You are so perfect and skinny. Same with Amara your perfect looking sister. And your cousins. Everyone is going to laugh at me and think I am so fat.* It will be so much fun. You have to come. You have to. Okay Kyla, well I don't know if I can. Like I said I have to ask my parents. *Besides I don't want to, I don't want to be seen in a bathing suit. If I was as perfect as you or your sister I wouldn't care. But I am so fat. I am so curvy. I don't want everyone to laugh at me.* I put on my bathing suit and looked at myself in the mirror. Fat thighs. Big boobs. *I wish I was perfect. I wish I was perfect. I wish I was perfect.*

*

REALITY. I never liked reality. Ever. Since the young age of nine, reality no longer really existed for me. I was living inside of my own world. A world filled with insecurities, self-doubt, anxiety and fear. A world that I was so convinced was a reality but it wasn't. It wasn't at all, because I was never living in the present moment.

ED was growing inside of me more and more each day.

GRADE EIGHT

November 22.1999

I am going to diet again. I've never really stuck to a diet before; I always quit. But at least now I have more of a goal. I am in a better dance school, I maybe have potential in the dance world, but I will never get anywhere if I am this fat. If my boobs are this big. My thighs are this thick. My hips are this wide. My butt is this large. I will never get anywhere in the dance world. I need to be flat. I need to be a more like a stick. Like every other girl in my dance class. I am in competition now. I don't want to be kicked out because I am too fat. I have to watch my weight. I am going to go to the library and get an actual diet book. I need to learn how to actually diet.

November 30.1999

I grabbed my little white book with pink hearts all over it and opened it up to the first page. I saw the information that I had entered from the last time I dieted and gave up. *Can I really do this, this time? I have already tried this thing two times. Well, whatever. It doesn't matter. This is a fresh start. Okay, so it is almost the day. I am going to lose all of my weight, my curves will shrink and then I will look like everyone else. I will be skinnier and be a better dancer, because dancers are supposed to be skinny. Now it is time to enter all of the important information.*

Current weight. 112. Last time I did this I was 107.

How have I gained weight? This isn't fair. Well I am glad that I am going on a diet again. Obviously it is needed. Obviously I just keep getting fatter and fatter. I think December 1st is a good time to start and that is tomorrow. I got this diet book from the library. I have never used one of these before – usually I just ate less and tried to make healthier choices. If I follow what this book says for a month I will lose all the weight I want. Twelve pounds isn't that much weight. This is going to be so easy. In one month, I will look like everyone else. By January 1st, 2000 my body will be like all the girls I want to look like. Thin legs. Small breasts. Tiny waist. I can't wait until I am no longer curvy. Until I am so skinny. Until I look absolutely perfect. I can't wait!

December 1.1999
Diet Day One:
I reached down into the cabinet. *The diet said that I can have one slice of whole wheat toast. It should be less than 100 calories.* I didn't know what a calorie meant. Didn't know how to measure where it was. *The book said to find the nutrition label on the food package.* I turned to the back of the bread bag. *Okay. I guess this is the nutrition box. Calories. Calories. Less than 100 calories. Where are they located?* I found

it; it was right at the top. *240 calories! Well that's too much. Is that just for one slice of bread? This sucks I will never lose weight now.* I looked back to the book. It said to make sure how much the calories were for. Trying to find the answer. Just above I located it – per two slices of bread. *Well that means that each slice of bread is 120 calories. That's too much. Well what else am I supposed to eat? That's all that I have.* I put the toast into the toaster. *This isn't right. This isn't right. You are going to eat too many calories. Well there is nothing else I can do. Maybe I'll just have three quarters then.* While I was waiting for the toast to be ready, I bent down and grabbed the peanut butter. I pulled open the drawer to my right and pulled out the first tablespoon that I could. I dug the big silver spoon into the tub. *It said one tablespoon right?* I looked over to the diet book. *How much should I eat again? Yeah, one tablespoon.* I pulled the spoon out of the jar and looked at it. *This is too much. But I want to eat it all. I normally eat it all. Well if I want to lose weight this is too much. One tablespoon.* I pulled open the drawer again and grabbed a butter knife. I began to scrape off the excess peanut butter to ensure that it only remained inside of the edges of the spoon. Because that's what one tablespoon was. Not anymore. Not anymore.

My toast had popped. I took it out. I grabbed a plate

and cut off one-quarter of the toast. *But I want to eat it all. Well you can't. You will never lose weight and have a perfect body if you don't follow what this diet says*. I threw the extra bread in the compost. Taking the butter knife I scraped out the peanut butter and spread it on the toast. *This is it? What else am I allowed to eat?* I looked back at the diet. *One cup of skim milk. I don't have skim milk. My parents don't buy that. Maybe I can just have a little and add water*. I poured two ounces of 2% milk into my glass, opened up the facet and filled the glass with water. I brought the cup to my mouth and began drinking. *Gross. This is disgusting*. I instantly threw it down the drain. *I guess I will just have normal milk, how much of a difference can it make?* I ate my toast while pacing back and forth through my kitchen. *What do I do? Do I give up? I'll just drink water. That's what I will do. Yeah I will just drink water instead*.

December 2.1999
Diet Day Two:
Today is day two of this diet. I am having a hard time following everything that it says considering more than half the food isn't in my house. I am going to try my best to follow what it says. I can always eat lots of fruit and vegetables if anything. Fruits and vegetables will not make me fat.

December 3.1999
Diet Day Three:
Okay its three days of this stupid diet. I want chips. I want chocolate. I want pasta. But I can't. I am not allowed. I am not allowed. My boobs are still big. Nothing is changing. Nothing is changing at all. This isn't going to work. What is the point of even trying? All of this food that I am told to eat I don't even have. My family doesn't eat this stuff. What am I supposed to eat for dinner? All my family is making is pasta. I guess I have to eat pasta then. I guess that means I am quitting this diet. Whatever it isn't like it is working anyways. I am never going to lose weight anyways. I guess I am not dieting anymore.
Christmas is in a few weeks, what is the point of trying to lose weight right now if I know I am just going to eat bad at Christmas anyways?

*

My girlfriends and I were all hard workers and very competitive with one another in a friendly type of way. We joined all of the groups and teams at school. By being this way it challenged me. Challenged me to keep up. To be part of the teams. But within my mind, I needed to be the best. I wanted to be the best. Yet, I never was. I would always compare myself to the other girls. I compared myself to their grades. To the shape of their bodies. To their hair color. Skin color. Eye color. Teeth size. To everything. Even though some of the girls at school were starting to look more like me it didn't matter. In my mind the girls who had hit puberty and developed like me were wrong as well. I was so fixated on the girls who hadn't developed yet and I wanted to look just like them. I was so convinced that if I had that type of body I would be a better dancer. I thought that if my body was like theirs the boys wouldn't be able to make fun of how big my breasts were. My mind changed even more so than it already had. A sea of insecurities continued to flood my mind daily and I had no idea of their effect on me.

*

August 12.2000

I looked up at the mirror in front of me. I stared at my reflection. *If they want me in competition again this means I am improving. Now they want me to compete in two groups.* I lifted up my shirt and looked at my stomach. *I need to lose weight. I need to shrink.* I looked down at my legs and grabbed my thighs. *Dancers don't have curves. Dancers are skinny.* I looked up at my breasts and grabbed them. *Dancers don't have big boobs like mine. My boobs are way too big to be a dancer.* I scanned my body up and down one more time. Tears began filling my eyes. Before I could begin to really cry my mind shifted. *Dieting is my answer. When I start school in September I am going to diet again. Yeah that will work; I am going to start dieting in September. I am going to high school anyways this year so this is a perfect time for a fresh start. I can't wait until I am skinny and look perfect.*

*

I had lots of friends when I began high school. Boys thought I was pretty. I seemed to have it all. I loved to dance. To socialize. I was always socializing. I would walk down the hallways at school. One of my friends was always by my side. I needed someone to always be by my side. A beaming smile was always on my face. I seemed happy. But it was shallow. It wasn't real. It wasn't authentic, but my smile still shone forward.

I would say hello to my schoolmates in the hall. Feeling wonderful that I was friends with so many of them. Feeling as if I was in some television show. A fairy tale. A story with happy endings. As if my life was some Disney movie. Some funny sitcom. On television shows things always seemed to work out perfectly. Seemed to end in a way that always worked out the way that they should. Perfectly. I wanted my life to be that way. Believed that my life would be that way.

Hoped that my life would be that way.

This is what I thought was real. But it wasn't. It wasn't at all. Yet, I didn't know this at all. The mere fact that I was faced with self-defeating thoughts each day, thoughts that put me down, made me feel inadequate. Always worrying about others. What they were thinking. What they were saying. Anxiety. Fears. This perfect world of mine did not exist at all. Yet, I thought these types of thoughts and the way I was, was normal.

I found myself through being around others. Having others to talk to. To turn to. When I talked to others I felt like I belonged. They wanted to be friends with me. This meant that I was okay. This gave me an identity. An identity of being a nice girl. A girl who got along with everyone. A girl who people liked.

I loved talking on the phone. I would spend each night talking on the phone from this friend to another friend. Hours would pass by. I would get a high off making the phone calls. It gave me a purpose. It gave me a feeling of belonging. People liked me and I liked them. This was my identity.

However, I didn't know any of this. I didn't know it at all. I just believed I liked others. Believed I was friends with everyone because I just liked people. And I did like people. I loved people. Yet, there were two reasons why I enjoyed talking to them so much. I wasn't really conscious of the second reason. I went from friend to friend. *Oh they like me. They want to spend time with me. Share their time with me.* I gained my self-esteem through being with others. Like a battery that needed to be re-charged in order to work again on full speed this is what I needed. I fed off being with others. Dove myself into each and every one of their worlds, where by being friends with them I found myself. Found how I should be. Took pieces of each of them and somehow incorporated all of those opinions into my own. I was like a chameleon. Not in a malicious way; this was rather automatic to me. I changed my way to suit whoever was in front of me. To fit in. To relate. To understand. To connect. I liked that I had so many close friends. Since so many people liked me, then that must mean I was a good person. That's at least what I thought.

I thought I was happy. And I was. On a superficial, phony level. Not superficial in the sense of materialistic things. Superficial in the sense of where my happiness came from. Doing.

My happiness came from doing things. Things that I thought I should be doing. It came from being a certain way. Being the person I thought I was. Being the person I thought I had to be. A perfect girl.

A perfect girl did not swear. She had to be nice. She had to be good with kids. She had to have a job. She had to be responsible. She had to get straight A's. She had to be a good friend. She had to be a good daughter. A good cousin. A good granddaughter. She had to be good at everything. Actually she had to be perfect at everything. This is who I thought I had to be. I had to be perfect.

Being perfect meant one thing to me. Being the best at everything. If I wasn't the best, I wasn't good enough. If I wasn't the best, I was wrong. If I wasn't the best, there was always room for improvement. My body wasn't the best. It wasn't perfect. Therefore, there was room for improvement. Luckily dieting still held all of the answers. At least that's what I thought.

*

GRADE TEN
October 20.2001
I stared at the naked reflection in front of me. Standing inside of my perfect pink and purple bedroom. I glanced over at the pictures that I had posted behind my bedroom wall. Countless images of perfect models

are hung there. Ten models in tiny white bikinis captured my eyes. I stared at them. I analyzed their bodies. *They are all so beautiful. They are all so perfect. Flat stomachs. Firm thighs. Tight butts. Narrow hips. Perfect breasts. Just perfect. Utterly perfect.*

I thought that having numerous pictures of skinny 'perfect' models in bikinis around me at all times would help motivate me to stay on track with my diet and body goals. I filled the back of my room door, my school agenda and even my school locker with these types of pictures, in hopes that they would somewhat force me to follow all of these diet rules perfectly. However, these pictures really did not work as a motivating force whatsoever. Seeing their 'perfect' bodies each and every day was a constant reminder of just how imperfect I felt my body was.

I looked back at myself. *My image is so imperfect. Flabby stomach. Fat thighs. Big bum. Wide hips. Huge breasts. Just imperfect. Utterly imperfect.* I grabbed a hold of my large breasts. I then grabbed my thighs. My ass cheeks. My stomach. My hips and then my breasts again. My mind whispered. *I hate them. I wish my boobs were smaller.* I dropped my breasts and stared at the image in front of me. I looked back at those perfect models. Before I turned back to the mirror my left hand grabbed hold of my left thigh from behind, getting a nice firm grip of all the inner flesh that I wished was never there. With my right hand I did the same thing with the right thigh, tightly pulling both pieces of meaty flesh away from one another, I am left standing in front of the mirror with only half of my thighs visible. My mind spoke a little louder, *This would be so much better; this is what I need to look like.* I pulled tighter. I stared deeper. My skin began to come loose from my right hand and my entire right thigh presented itself to me. *F-A-T.* I looked at my left thigh, the one that I was still holding onto firmly. The one that was missing half of what really belonged to it. *That's better, that's perfect. But that's not my thigh.* I instantly dropped my left hand and stared at my naked body in the mirror. *Ugly. Fat. Disgusting. Imperfect. Fat. Fat. Nasty. Disgusting. Fat. Imperfect. Utterly Imperfect. I just want to eat. I just want to eat. It's too late now. In order to lose weight you need to not eat three hours before you go to bed. I read that in one of my diets. Don't eat. Do not eat. Eating this late is bad.* My mind started racing as these thoughts continue. *I'm so ugly. I'm so fat. My boobs are too big. My thighs are too thick. My hips are too wide. My butt is too large. I have been dieting off and on since I was in grade six. What the fuck is the matter with me? Why can't I just lose the weight? It's not that hard. I am such a loser. I am such a failure. Well this is it. I have to lose it now. I just have to. I am so fat. I have to lose weight.* I could no longer look at my own reflection anymore as I was utterly disgusted by what I saw. *I am going to start dieting on November 1st. Yeah that makes the most sense. Then I will lose weight. I just have to. I just have to. I can't be like this anymore.*

*

Dieting off and on for as long as I did at that point not only affected my way of thinking towards my body, my weight and my appearance, but it also had a huge impact on the way in which I began thinking about the rest of the world around me.

Alongside my list of rules which I had unconsciously made for myself to follow in order to be perfect, continuing to diet for so long began altering and manipulating my everyday thought processes. As a result of living my everyday life according to a list of rules, I started to develop an "either-or" mentality.
If you really think about how diets are presented to us, it is quite easy to recognize how this sort of thinking could occur. The absolute precision that is required in order to follow a plan one-hundred percent accurately is very hard to do, especially as a pre-teen or teenager. Parties, hanging out with friends, or the plain fact that my parents were constantly preparing, watching and

commenting on everything that I ate, always made whatever diet I was on impossible for me to follow perfectly – and of course, unless I followed it perfectly, I was a failure.

By now I was so used to judging myself according to a particular scale in relation to my body shape, weight and what I ate that this was simply a normal way of thinking for me. My initial "either or" mentality relating to food and exercise began overshadowing numerous other areas of my life. Places where I actually was succeeding were beginning to suffer. I began being unable to take pleasure in many of my accomplishments in school or in dance class, as nothing I ever did seemed quite good enough anymore. Rather than focusing on all of the things that I did well, my mind became fixated on how I could have done them all so much better.

This type of thinking – that I was either doing something perfectly or else there was no point in doing it at all – would later result in destroying many other areas of my life. Yet, like everything occurring during my life throughout this time, it was all taking place unconsciously. At the time, I simply thought that I had found the answer to how I could lose weight which in turn would make me become the perfect person that I was so convinced I needed to be. However, because

I could never quite get my body to look just like those 'perfect' models' bodies I was surrounded by at all times, I believed that I was missing out on all of the personal happiness that would occur if I obtained a perfect body like theirs.

I was so convinced that continuing to diet was the best way to achieve my status of perfection. Nothing could have been further from the truth.

*

May 28.2002

I seemed secure. I seemed confident. On the outside. I walked down the runway with a beaming smile on my face. *I hope people don't think my legs are too fat. I hope they aren't laughing at how big my boobs are.* I walked up the stairs located on the right hand side of the stage. With a smile on my face, I put my left hand on my left thigh. *If I put my hand here, it will cover the biggest part of my thigh. That means people don't have to see how fat it is.* No one would have noticed this. No one would have noticed this at all. Yet, I knew. I knew what I was doing. Trying to cover my thighs from the audience.

*

I was convinced that I was the only one who felt this

way. The only one who was insecure. Everyone else seemed so sure of themselves, so confident and happy. Put together. I took them all at face value, believing whoever someone presented themselves to be was who they were.

This played a huge part in why I continued to take other people's opinions as the truth. I was never sure of anything. Could always be persuaded both ways. Never really formulated an opinion of my own. Therefore those around me who seemed the most sure, seemed like they knew what they were talking about were always right in my mind. More importantly, I continued to let other people's opinion as to who I was play a huge, if not the entire role, in how I defined myself.

*

July 14.2002
I get out of bed. All of my friends are still sleeping. We had a sleepover last night. I walk into the kitchen and open up the fridge. *Oh, I am so thirsty.* I see orange juice. *Oh that's healthy; I'll have a big glass of that.* I pour myself a glass and down it. Then I pour myself another glass and sit at the table. Some of the girls walk into the kitchen and say hello. Kyla, Renee, Maija and Ashley sit down at the table. Maijia pulls

out the orange juice and plops it down on the table. The nutrition label is facing directly at me. *Oh, I didn't know they would make one of those things for orange juice. I thought they only made that for foods.* I look at it. *110 calories. OMG! I didn't think that juice had that many calories. OMG! I can't believe I just drank two glasses of that. What a waste. I could have eaten something. Now I already started off the day wrong. Now I already put like over 200 calories into my body and I haven't even had breakfast yet. Why didn't I just choose water? I need to drink eight glasses of water a day anyways; I remember reading that in one of my diets. Why didn't I just have water instead? I am such an idiot.* The girls kept talking. I smile and act as if I am really engaged in the conversation but every time someone else is talking I stare back at the nutrition label. *110 calories. I am such an idiot. 110 calories. I guess I am not starting perfect today. I am such an idiot. I am never going to lose weight today. I already messed up.*

There are chips laid out on the counter. Ashley pulls the bag down and starts eating a few. Then Renee. She offers me some. *No I shouldn't eat that.* No thanks. *They are bad. Besides I said today was going to be the day I started fresh. Started eating perfectly and chips are certainly not considered perfect.* I am staring at them. Then I see Kyla start eating some of the pretzels. *Well maybe I can eat that. Pretzels are*

*better than chips I guess. I already fucked up any-
ways. I already had two big glasses of orange juice
the day is already ruined.* Can I have some? Kyla
gives me the bag. At this point we are all munching on
chips and pretzels while talking about our night last
night. Everyone is laughing and so am I. But inside I
am fighting something. *I might as well just eat them.
I just want chips too. If all the girls are eating them
and they stay this skinny, then maybe it won't really
affect me either. Regardless, I will just start fresh
and perfect tomorrow. I will definitely not be drinking orange juice that's for sure. Tomorrow I will eat
perfectly*

*

I thought I was happy. And I was. On a superficial,
phony level. Not superficial in the sense of materialistic things. Superficial in the sense of the level of
my happiness. Shallow. My level of happiness was
so shallow. My lack of authenticity caused this pat-
tern. By engaging in things I thought I "should" be
doing. Acting in ways I thought I "should" be acting. I
was searching for happiness derived from places that
didn't stem or initiate from myself. Happiness from
external sources. There was no happiness that truly
stemmed from me. It was all external. It was all shallow. I thought that these external things were what
was bringing me happiness and would continue to

bring me happiness. But I was wrong. I had no idea. Shallow forms of happiness always lead to break-downs, as they aren't real. Shallow forms of happiness always break. They always break.

*

REALITY. I couldn't handle reality. I couldn't handle all of the differences. The anxiety. The fear. The constant comparisons. The way in which I was constantly criticizing myself. My insecurities, which began at the young age of nine, now formed together to create a story about who I thought I was, which I now fully believed. My story went like this.

I am imperfect. I need to be fixed. Changed. Altered. I am different and being different is bad. Being different results in people to laugh at me. Comment on my appearance. Make fun of my differences. Standing out is bad. Fitting in is good. Boys only like me because of my breasts. My breasts are way too big, they need to be smaller. Once I lose weight, lose my curves, I will fit in. Until then I am imperfect. Losing weight is my answer and dieting is my means to get there. Unless I am on a diet I won't be a good dancer. Unless I am on a diet, I am not good enough. Unless I am dieting I am wrong. My body must look like my friends' bodies. My body must look like a typical

*dancer's body, therefore not allowed to have curves.
My breasts must be smaller than those of all adults
or anyone older than me. I must eat each portion that
is outlined to me in that diet at every meal. I must
drink a minimum of eight glasses of water a day. I
must not eat three hours before I go to bed. I must try
to not eat carbs or junk food ever and if I do certainly
don't have them for dinner. I must always work out
in the morning before I have had anything to eat
to burn the most fat. If I don't follow these rules, I
am wrong, I am bad, I am not perfect. I need to lose
weight. I need to be perfect.*

I hope that up to this point, you can see how I interpreted all of these experiences. I added meaning to
each instance, defining each moment to indicate a
part of who I was. I was attached to these experiences,
believed these experiences held the absolute truth.
Yet, the truth was ED was with me every step of the
way during this time but I had no idea. Like an MP3
player that played the same songs automatically on repeat, ED just continued replaying the story of who he
believed I was. I just assumed whatever I was thinking
about myself was the truth.

You may be wondering why I am sharing all of this personal information with you, especially after asking you
so many personal questions about yourself. To be hon-

est, in the first draft of this book I didn't have any of my personal experiences added in this book. I wanted the book to be about you, presenting you with exercises and explanations for how you can begin to truly fall in love with yourself, your body and your life. Yet, my editor and publisher really felt that by sharing some of my own experiences with you it would help showcase how these exercises worked for me and I couldn't agree with them more.

My goal in sharing my experiences with you is to possibly help spark experiences and events from your own life. Experiences that you may have forgotten about, ignored, learned how to deal with or pretended didn't affect you. The truth is that our past experiences highly affect who we think we are and how we currently see ourselves today. I will get into the importance that our pasts play in our lives later on in this book. As for now, I would like to share a little bit more about my past with you, as my story of who ED convinced me to believe I was didn't stop at the age of sixteen. As I grew older, the way in which I interpreted and attached myself to the different experiences I went through, or should I say the way that ED convinced me to see these experiences, resulted in additional information to be added to the story of who I believed that "this Paula" was.

Here is another glimpse into some other experiences

that led my story to include the following beliefs:

I am so fat. I am unlovable. I am dumb. I am ugly. I am not good enough. I need to be perfect. I need to have a perfect body. When I have a perfect body, my boyfriend and I will be back to what we used to be. I need to have my boyfriend in my life. He is the only guy for me. I cannot be alone. I don't know who I am without my friends or my boyfriend. My friends never cared about me. I can never say no. I must always wear a smile on my face and act like everything is fine. I need to lose weight.

GRADE ELEVEN
November 15.2002
Should I get that? I don't know what I want. Maybe this? I don't know. Should I get that? I don't know what I want. What if I order something and it's bad? I don't know what I want. I just wish someone would choose for me. I don't know. I don't know. "Hmm, what should I eat? What are you getting?" *I'll just get whatever he gets.* He decided on Chinese food, so I followed. We sat down across from one another at the local mall food court. This was the first time we had been alone together outside of school. I was nervous. So nervous. He kept staring at me. He was staring at me with that gaze. That gaze that he always seemed to give me lately. *Why does he keep looking and smiling*

*at me like that? I feel uncomfortable, is there some-
thing in my teeth?*

*Okay... just eat your food. Yeah I know, but he keeps
looking at me. What if I get food on my face and I
look stupid? Shit! How am I not going to get noodles
all over my face? I always make a mess. I don't want
him to see that I can't eat perfectly.* I put my hand up
in front of my mouth. "What are you doing?" He said.
We both started laughing. Then while giggling I said,
"I don't like having people watch me when I eat, don't
look at me, okay?" He said okay. I looked down and
continued eating. *I really hope he stops looking at
me. I hope he doesn't think I am fat. I hope he doesn't
think I am ugly. I hope he doesn't think I am gross.*
I put my hand down and looked up. He was staring
at me, with that same gaze in his eyes. That gaze he
always seemed to give me. I smiled. I was nervous. So
nervous. I smiled.

February 15.2003
We had only been dating for just about three months
now, but I had known him since grade two. This was
the boy I spoke about earlier, the only one I ever felt
liked me for me. Over the last few months, he had
gotten to know me better than anyone else did. He
could see me. The real me. But he could also still see
the part of me that was controlled by ED. At the young

age of sixteen, he was able to see what was behind all of my insecurities. He told me that I had no idea who I was. That I was misled. That I was mistaken. He had no idea that ED was in my life, but could see the way that ED made me talk and think about myself.

He was right, I had no clue who I really was, yet I didn't really understand him at first. I thought I knew who I was. I was a sixteen year old girl who loved to dance, hang out with my friends, was from an Italian family, wanted to be a teacher and was in grade eleven. I thought this was who I was. Yet, I had no idea.

We continued talking. By the end of the conversation, I knew he was right. I didn't really know who I was. I just somewhat had an idea about myself. These things were all related to externals. To the shallows, like the activities that I enjoyed doing.

I had never thought of any of this before that moment. He was able to bring the real me to the forefront. He was the only one. By the end of this conversation we both decided that me knowing myself was very important. This was important not only for me but also if we wanted to be together. I looked him in the eyes and smiled. My heart fluttered. My breathing fastened. I had made a decision. At that very moment I made a decision. Now was the time for me to embark upon a journey. Now was the time for me to start my journey where I was searching for something important. Something huge. Something I had no idea how to find. Myself. This is where my journey truly began.

February 17.2003

I am starting this diary in search for myself. I am sick of being the way I am and doing the things I do. Also my self-confidence and negative thoughts are constantly on my mind and I know that I am better than them. I want to find out who I am, the real me. I want to be confident and stop thinking so negatively because it is wasting so much time. I just don't know how to do this. How can I change my thoughts? I once saw or heard that writing down your feelings is one way of dealing and facing them. So I guess that is what I am going to do. I am doing this for myself but also for him. I am falling in love and that scares me. I know it shouldn't but it does. Like once I am truly in love there's no turning back, right? At least if I am not fully there then I can't get hurt. I don't want to be hurt and left all alone when I know I need that person in my life but they leave. He said he will never leave me but one day he will get sick of me and want someone better...I need to take those negative thoughts and cover them up with positive ones that I have. I know I have them, I just don't think they are right, but I am going to try because I promised him and myself that I would. Feeling confused about a lot of things is not a good thing for me. I hate it, this is something I need to fix and this is my journey to do so. This is a soul search were I am going to find out who I really am.

*

I started this journey just a month shy of my seventeenth birthday. I didn't fully understand what 'finding myself' meant. I didn't realize that this was something that could not be forced. I didn't realize that this was something that could not be found within a week or two. There was no book that I could buy. Course that I could take. Video that I could watch. There was no quick fix that would allow me to find myself. That would give me a direct approach to find myself. I was so lost. I really had no idea where to begin. Yet, I didn't know this. It was the result of my complete lack of personal awareness. My lack of where I was headed next.

But, week by week things were changing. Everything was about to change. From this day forward things would never be the same. A breakdown was waiting for me just around the corner. So I did what I had been doing for years. I wrote in my journal. Rather than writing about the latest gossip from school, I wrote about myself. I wrote about this change. I wrote about falling in love for the first time. I wrote about him. I wrote about us. I wrote about why I wanted to find myself. For him. For me. For us. I wrote. I didn't have the slightest idea what I was going to find out about myself through my words.

*

February 18.2003
He said he wanted me to tell him why he loves me and I told him that I don't have any reason why he loves me. I am not used to writing or thinking about my good qualities so this might take a while. Ummm, I don't know, I guess I will think harder. Okay good things about me inside and out against the bad. I guess I will start with the good on the outside.

Hair: wish it was straighter
Eyebrows: nice when waxed
Eyes: favorite quality
Nose: all right, kinda fat, nice from side
Teeth: disgusting, color is gross
Smile: nice sometimes, other times too big
Face Skin: could be a lot better, lately I have been getting pimples
Ears: whatever
Boobs: nice in clothes sometimes, ugly without
Stomach: sometimes I like it, except when I am bloated and I hate the side (love handles)
Arms: too hairy and red stuff is ugly

Fingers: I am actually beginning to not care
Thighs: nasty (upper) fat, cellulite (lower) could be nice
but I don't really care same with calves
Butt: sometimes nice in pants, too big and fat in thongs,
cellulite
Ankles: boney but whatever
Feet/toes: ugly but beginning to accept them a little more
Overall Body Skin: alright except for on my thighs, butt
and upper arms

*

No one else knew I felt this way about myself. I was so
used to acting this way, trying to be perfect in everything that I did. Putting on that smile. It all seemed
normal. Yet, when I was with him something happened. Something changed. Just like everyone else
around me, he saw me differently than I saw myself.
He told me how he felt about me all the time. Yet, just
like what I did with everything, I didn't believe him.
I never truly believed him. I could not wrap my head
around how he could possibly love me. I felt that I was
just impossible to love. I didn't know this at the time,
but I felt this way because I did not love myself.

*

February 25.2003

As I would walk down the hall with him by my side, I smiled. I seemed happy. From the outside. And I was on a shallow level. *Everyone thinks my thighs are fat. Everyone thinks my boobs are too big and ugly. Everyone thinks my hips are too wide. Everyone thinks I am fat.* These thoughts would repeat in my mind with every step I took. I would look over to him and smile on the outside. *I don't understand how he wants to be with me. Why he wants to be with me. He is a star athlete. He is one of the hottest guys in our school. He is fit. Strong. Handsome. Popular. He can get lots of girls. Lots of them. But he chose to be with me. Why? I am not the prettiest. I am not the smartest. I don't have the best body. And I certainly am not the skinniest. Why does he still want to be with me?* He would lean in and kiss me. My mind would be silent for a split second. After he pulled his lips off of mine, my mind would go back. *Fat. Big boobs. Thick thighs. Wide Hips. Fat. Big boobs. Thick thighs. Wide Hips. Fat. Big boobs. Thick thighs. Wide Hips. Why does he still want to be with me?*

March 8.2003

Today is my second day of vacation and I am having such a great time! I really need to change my ways and some of the things I do not like about myself. I pray to God that I can change those things about me but (1) I don't know how and (2) Where do I begin? (3) How long is this going to take? Because if I cannot change some of my ways I probably cannot have the love I truly want. I am going to write about all of the good qualities about me and the bad ones inside and out. I already did the outside ones and from that I can conclude that I am happy with myself except for my thighs, butt, tummy (sides) and my teeth. So I think if I do lose a lot of weight and get that surgery on my teeth, I will have a lot more confidence that will help me a lot with other things. Now I know I still have to list all the good and bad qualities about me inside but I will do that another day, I want to write down thing I MUST do to improve.

1) The way that I care about what other people think about me
2) My weight
3) My teeth
4) The way in which I am always want to and need to be the best at everything: looks, school, dance etc
5) The way in how I sometimes try to get compliments from others, when in reality I should only care about the people who love me

Overall, I am going to try my best to improve these things about me.

March 9.2003
I have noticed a few things about myself from this vacation. I ALWAYS think about food and my body (99.9% are bad thoughts) and usually about what others are thinking or saying about me and I hate it. I am constantly comparing myself to others (their bodies) and I need to change that. Also it's like I have to constantly be doing something so I really don't get to sit down and think about myself. I know that when I go back to school, I am going to try my best to change.

March 10.2003
Right now I am sitting on the beach, it's so beautiful. The reason I am writing at this moment is because (1) I am by myself, so it's a lot easier and (2) because as I am writing, when I am on the beach, it lets me think differently than I would, let's say in my bedroom. I want to tell this diary that I am very determined to change certain things about me. I think losing weight will help me A LOT; so when I get back I will be seventeen years old, since Friday is my birthday and that's when I am going to start my life. For me and for the people I love. I hope, actually, I know I am going to be able to do it, it's going to be hard work though but it will all be worth it when I am skinny and look perfect.

*

By writing that I was determined to change, my real self shone through. I didn't need anything. I didn't have to do anything. I was just determined. Driven. Wanting to be a better girl. A better person. There were no shallows here. Simply authenticity. Yet, by the stroke of that next sentence, this determination was overtaken by a shallow quality. An external yard-stick.

You can think of these external shallow points that I keep referring to as an indication that ED was around. ED was formulated in the shallows. ED was the one who was convincing me that my body needed to change a lot. It was as if my life wouldn't start until this change occurred. Waiting for my life to begin meant that I was never truly living in the present moment. ED did not know how to let me live in the present moment. ED did not know how to survive in the present moment. ED only survived through feeding me the story about who he thought I was. The story about how "this Paula" needed to be skinnier, look and be perfect. As a result, of listening to ED's story I was always missing out on whatever moment I was living in. I wasn't free now. I wasn't real now. I wasn't being self-expressive now. I wasn't exuding self-love now. I wasn't being anything or anyone like I was when I was a child, because I always seemed to be waiting for something to happen to change it all. Yet that something never came.

*

March 22.2003
Plaid skirt, white shirt, grey knee highs. I had come straight from school with Justin and Helena to sign up for Weight Watchers. *This is the perfect answer for me. Clearly there is something wrong with me if I have been trying to lose weight for over six years and I can't seem to keep it off. Weight Watchers will help me I just know it.* I walked into the room and signed up. *I can't wait until I am skinny and look perfect. Then I will look better for him. I can't wait until I am skinny.*

April 22.2003
I'm going to my cousin's wedding on Saturday. It's Tuesday now. There is tons of food at weddings. So much food. It tastes so good. I have to eat it all. I can't not eat the food that is served at the wedding. I don't want to not eat all the food that's at the wedding. I am going to mess up my diet. I am going to eat bad food. I might as well eat chips and cookies and ice cream tonight. I might as well enjoy everything until then. I will never eat this food again. So I might as well. I will eat perfectly after the wedding. After the wedding I will eat perfectly. I just have to.

Then I will become skinny and look perfect.

*

All ED convinced me to care about was trying to look perfect and become skinny. I was still simply trying to fill a role that I believed I had to fill; be the most perfect girl in the world. Filing this role meant everything to me, because without being perfect in everything that I did, who was I? Unless I was perfect, I was a nobody. Unless I was perfect, I wasn't worth anything. Unless I was perfect, no one would ever really love me.

The truth was unless I was perfect according to what I believed a perfect person should consist of, act like, behave like and look like I didn't consider myself worthy of being truly loved the way I wanted to be loved by Justin or anyone. This all took place unconsciously of course, as I surely didn't choose to think that I wasn't deserving of having any type of self-trust, self-acceptance, self-love and self-knowledge. Yet, ED was so good at convincing me that I didn't deserve any love of any kind that I believed I truly didn't deserve any of it until I was perfect.

*

June 20.2003

Image

Don't like what I see

Yet I can't do anything about it

Takes work and self-discipline to achieve success

I just feel as though there is no point

It makes me feel good, but after I end up just feeling like shit

I am realizing I want it for myself but that's obviously not enough

I want it for him

To have him look at me with the look that he is proud and honored to be with me, not ashamed

It's like I end up feeling sorry for myself and do it just because it comforts me

I need to take control of my life and start to realize that I control everything, when it comes to this

I make decisions, I just don't know how to get the thoughts out of my head, it's like they are always on my mind, truly pathetic and disgusting

It's like more than half of the time I give in, and when I don't I am like going insane

What's wrong with me?

Why do I feel this way?

I want to look good but it's like when I see it that thought goes away

I realize I am not doing it for me anymore

It's all about him

Because I have been trying for myself for a long time but nothing seems to work
I am giving myself three months
Three months to see change
I know it's going to take time
But the final result is going to be worth it
After the first two weeks I better keep going because I can never seem to get past it
I can do it
And I am starting tomorrow
Every day I am going to write
And at the end of the three months
I will show him it all
And I hope he is proud
I am doing it for him now, because I think that will help me
I love him and want him to be proud and not be embarrassed

*

I no longer felt like he loved me like he once did, as our relationship had gone through numerous changes and faced many issues. I still yearned for that love that he gave me at the beginning. I wanted that love. Felt like I needed that love.

I had no idea that ED had added Justin into the story

about who I was. My boyfriend had now become a part of my identity. I began doing things for him, as I had no idea how to really do anything for myself. Since couldn't seem to gain control of losing weight for myself, I began focusing on him. I claimed that I wanted to receive acceptance from him. That I wanted him to be proud of me. That I wanted him to not be embarrassed by the person that I was. Yet, the truth was that I didn't accept myself, I wasn't proud of myself and I was embarrassed of the person that I was.

Once again, I didn't realize any of this at the time, so I continued focusing on the external. On the shallow. On ways to change myself. To alter. To fix. To give me what I thought I really wanted. To change me into who ED convinced me that I had to be in order for him to love me like he once did. In my mind all of this was affected and could be controlled by my weight. By my body. By what I looked like. All of it. When I looked perfect, he would love me like he used to.

Or so ED convinced me.

As my own insecurities rose, I changed. Changed into exactly who ED was telling me I was. My attitude was different. I was negative. I was sad. I was unsure. I was quiet. I was depressed. Yet, he stayed around.

He knew how much I needed him. He knew that he couldn't abandon me. Yet, by staying around my attachment to him only increased. My dependency amplified. My desire to have him stay around forever escalated. I found myself through his presence, his opinion, his perception of who I was. I had lost myself completely into the hands of another. I lost myself inside of us.

I didn't choose this; there was no choice in the matter. Absolutely no choice in the matter. I hid behind him. I liked it there. It was safe. It was known. It was out of my control. It was all in his hands. Yet, day after day, week after week, the image of who I looked at in the mirror was changing very quickly.
The girl that he was dating was changing. The girl that he fell in love with was no longer there. No longer was I the Paula that he promised always and forever to.

I was a different girl. I was now entirely controlled by ED. No longer did he only see ED from time to time; ED embodied a majority of my day. Like I was possessed by something that was extremely dark, scary and extremely insecure. The thoughts that I was thinking were no longer mine. They were all ED's. I was no longer there. I was nowhere to be found. I was completely lost.

*

GRADE TWELVE

Since the young age of nine, I never loved myself fully and because of this no one ever stood a chance of really loving me the way they might have wanted to. The way that I even knew that I wanted to be loved. Until I would learn to love myself, I was never going to love anyone else the way they deserved either. That love that I now exuded to Justin got mixed up with approval. With EGO. With wanting to receive an equal amount of love in return. With power. Ultimately with ulterior motives.

Real love doesn't work that way. Real love is selfless. Authentic love does not want anything except to love. However, shallow forms of love are always attached to something more. They are always linked to ulterior motives. They are attached to the outcome; if that love is not granted in return, the person shuns or cries or pulls away or hurts or wants revenge as if something was taken from them. By giving another their love they lost part of themselves; they gave too much of themselves.

I did exactly this. I gave my entire self to him. All of me. The bad. The good. There were no boundaries established whatsoever. I unleashed all of my energy, all of my emotions, all of my heart into his hands. He was responsible for all of it now. All of it. I constantly felt as if there was something inside of me that needed to be filled up. He was supposed to be able to fill that void for me; to make me feel love.

There were many times when I felt that I didn't get that love or attention from him. I would be left in a negative state, sitting inside of uncomfortable feelings. I could not stand these feelings and did not know how to deal with them. There was something inside of me that was missing. Food was something I could use to fill that void. To numb those uncomfortable feelings. Food was always there. Always.

*

A breakdown was no longer waiting for me just around the corner. I had spotted it. And it had spotted me. I had walked straight into it and it had hit me like a pile of bricks, crashing down one-by-one onto my life. My insecurities increased enormously. My anxiety levels sky-rocketed. My determination to find out who I was lost all of its power. Just six months before this, six little months before, I was determined to discover who I was. To become this powerful woman that I truly wanted to be. But now I was broken. I was sad. I didn't mean for things to turn out this way. Yet, there was nothing that I believed I could do to change things. Day by day I began fading away. Day by day things were changing.

*

October 8.2003
It was lunch time. I had second period lunch. Justin had first. I had no one to hang out with, since my friends and I were no longer talking based on a big miscommunication which had taken place the year before. This broke my heart and was another reason why ED's presence, along with my attachment to him increased.

I was alone now during lunch times. My mom would pack lunches for me. Boring. Somewhat healthy. But not enough. It was never enough. Each lunch period was a reminder to me just how much of a loser I was. That I was alone. That no one understood me.

I sat at my locker. Had my homework on one side. My boring lunch on the other. I stared down at my homework. I was focused. About thirty seconds later the page became a blur.

Everyone thinks you are such a loser. Who eats lunch by themselves? I can't believe I am not friends with the girls anymore. How did this happen? They don't care about me. They never cared about me. Our whole friendship was a lie. I have no friends. No one understands me. I don't want to be here anymore. I am such a loser. I have no friends.

As these thoughts continued I inhaled my lunch.

More. I want more.

It wasn't enough. It was never enough.

More. More. Go get those fries downstairs. And a cookie. They will make you feel better. More. More. I shouldn't though. I am going to get fatter.

I stared down at the page. Tried to re-focus. To re-gain some control. My mind was racing. My heart was pounding.

Loser. No friends. Nobody likes you. Loser. Loner. No friends. Eat. Food. More. Eat. Food. More. The fries will make you feel better. They taste so good. I just won't eat for the rest of the day. I just can't eat for the rest of the day.

I got up from the cold ground. Put my books back into my locker. I grabbed a sweater and some money and started heading downstairs.

Which is the fastest route to get me there? I am not going to go through the front corridor. I don't want people to see that I am alone. I wish I didn't have to walk downstairs by myself. I am such a loser. I have no friends. Who eats lunch by themselves? Me.

I headed down the stairs, made a quick right turn down the hall. Another quick left and then a right. I was about to enter the cafeteria. It was filled with people. None of my old friends were usually ever in there. They were always across the street. I wished I was with them across the street too. Like I used to be.

Worrying. Nervous. Unsure. I took a deep breathe. *Just don't look at anyone. Just walk into the part where they sell food. Ready. Go.*

I opened the door and walked straight in. Fear. Embarrassment. Shame. I avoided looking at everyone. I didn't want to see them. I didn't want them to see me. I was too broken. Too screwed up. Didn't want to put on a fake face any more than I felt I had to. I made a quick right turn and entered the part of the cafeteria where they served food. French fries. Chocolate chip cookies.

Which one should I get? I shouldn't be buying this. I shouldn't be buying this. I am going to get so fat. Well

I am already down here. I am already fat anyways. Who cares? This will make you feel better when you eat it. I just can't eat for the rest of the day. I just can't eat for the rest of the day. Just shut up and eat it. It will make you feel better. Should I get both? Or just the fries? Or just a cookie? Both? Or one?

I gave in. Like every other time. Almost every single lunch hour that I actually stayed at school for. Sometimes I would get both. Depending on how shitty I felt. Depending on what day of my diet that I was on. Depending on a number of factors. Him. Me. Encounters with the girls. Sadness. Anxiety. Fear. It was all based on that. How much I ate was always based on my emotional status of that day. Yet, I had no idea how to control or change things.

I quickly rushed out of the cafeteria. Trying to avoid all those people as fast as I could. I headed back to my locker alone. All alone.

Things are so different now. Things are so different. I hate it here. I hate it here. I don't belong. I don't belong. I am such a loser. I hate myself. I have no friends. Everyone hates me. I am so fat. I am so gross. I am such a loser.

My mind would repeat these thoughts. Over and over and over again. As I headed back to my locker I tried to avoid making eye contact with anyone.

OMG, everyone sees how fat I am. And that I am buying these fries. Thank God I hid the cookie in my sweater pocket. No one knows that I ate the lunch my mom packed me already. So eating these fries is normal. Eating these fries is normal.

I made it back. I instantly felt relieved. Didn't have to walk around anymore by myself. I opened up my locker and grabbed my books. I closed my locker door. My back was against it. I slid right down. Spread my legs out in front of me. My fries on one side. My books on the other. My cookie was hiding in my pocket.

I can't believe I just bought this shit. I am so fat. I am such a loser. I am disgusting. I cannot eat for the rest of today. I cannot.

I opened up a textbook and started reading. About two sentences in, my mind would go back. *I am such a loser. I hate myself. I have no friends. Everyone hates me. I am so fat. I am so gross. Who eats lunch by themselves in front of their locker? I am such a loser.*

These thoughts would continue over and over and over again. I listened. I then started eating fry after fry after fry. Those voices were so mean. Always put me down. I didn't know how to deal with it. The only thing that seemed to help was food. Food seemed to make things a bit better. Allowing myself to momentarily slip away. Momentarily.

I hope no one sees me eating these. It's perfect because no one is up here. I wouldn't want people to see me eating these fries again. I eat them so much. Eat. More. Faster. More. Faster. Make sure no one sees you eating these.

When I was done eating the thoughts came back louder and meaner than ever. *You fat piece of shit. Look what you just did. You keep gaining weight. Yet, you continue to keep eating this way. No shit you are fat. What's wrong with you?*

Guilt. Shame. Embarrassment. I tried to continue reading but I couldn't focus. My thoughts kept beating me down.

You are such a loser. Who eats lunch by themselves? Who eats lunch by themselves? I can't believe you just ate all that. Who eats a lunch and then fries? And you have a cookie to eat too! You are such a loser. More. Eat. More. You already ate all of those fatty fries. You might as well eat your fatty cookie too. You better not eat for the rest of today. You fat idiot. You better not eat anymore today.

I reached into my pocket for my cookie. I broke off a piece. With that first bite pleasure took over me. Soft dough. Sweet chocolate. Made me instantly feel good; get an instant sense of happiness throughout myself. This sense of pleasure lessoned with the second bite. Was barely there by the third. Was completely gone by the fourth. Guilt. Shame. Embarrassment.

This sense of pleasure was replaced by thoughts loudly screaming in my mind. These extremely abusive, self-defeating, self-harming thoughts were all stemming from ED, yet I had no idea.

You fat piece of shit. What did you just do? I can't believe you just ate fries and a cookie and you already ate the lunch your mom packed for you! Are you really that stupid? If you eat like this you are going to keep getting fatter. No kidding you're a loser. No kidding you have no friends. No kidding you and him aren't getting along like you used to. Look at you. You are so pathetic. So pathetic. You have absolutely no control over yourself. No control. Fat idiot.

My eyes started tearing up. *I can't cry. I can't cry. I miss my friends. I miss my friends. I didn't mean for things to turn out this way. But they don't care about*

me anymore. They probably never did. I want to get out of here. I can't be here anymore. I can't. Eat. More. Food. Eat. More. Food. Eat. More. Food.
I wanted to go home. There was tons of food in my fridge. My house was always stocked with food. I wanted to go home. I wanted more. I needed more. Always needed more.

*

December 15.2004
With every bite ED appears. *You shouldn't be eating this. Why are you eating this? This is fatty. This isn't good.* I eat as fast as I can. As if I am trying to run away from those thoughts in my mind. Bite after bite ED comments. *You are fat. You are fat. This is so good. This is so good.* I look down, my plate is empty. *OMG, why did I just eat that!?! I am so fat. I am so fat. I might as well eat more.* This had been happening for years. This was just my normal relationship with food. My normal relationship with my body. My normal relationship with myself. ED had taken over and convinced me that this was the only way I could be.

February 1.2004
This book says that I am going to have to start writing in a journal so I will do so here. I realized that I always look

at people and what they look like, what they are wearing and whether their bodies are skinnier or fatter than mine. I realized that is so stupid. So this time when I automatically wanted to do that I said DON'T, so I didn't. The feeling of confidence and approval came over me saying, "Wow you can actually not care about others." Evidently I truly do care what they think of me. Anyways, I feel good, I tested myself. Could I handle being criticized or rejected??? That's a good question for me.

May I feel calm. May I feel peace. May I feel relaxed.

I want to be confident in both my looks and thoughts and not care about others opinions of me.
I want to be confident in both my looks and thoughts and not care about others opinions of me.
I want to be confident in both my looks and thoughts and not care about others opinions of me.
I want to be confident in both my looks and thoughts and not care about others opinions of me.
I want to be confident in both my looks and thoughts and not care about others opinions of me.
I want to be confident in both my looks and thoughts and not care about others opinions of me.
I want to be confident in both my looks and thoughts and not care about others opinions of me.
I want to be less loud (quieter)
I want to stop interrupting people
I want to stop thinking negatively

I want to enjoy every minute of every day and live life to the fullest
I want to relax
I want to have fun

*

I believed that having a trainer, who could help me attain my perfect body would allow me to find happiness that I needed. She not only became my trainer, but she was also becoming a close friend as every session she heard my problems, the unleashing of my life into her hands. I was just yearning for someone to connect with, begging for someone to understand me and praying that someone would love me to make up for my lack of self-love.

*

February 10.2004
I need to connect with myself, I think I should start taking yoga classes, once a week, to learn how to relax and also for something to do. I want to be who I know I can be; I guess I just have to keep testing myself. So I am going to make a weekly schedule of workouts, dance, yoga and reading at night that I must follow to make sure I'm getting enough time in for myself.

February 10.2004
Mirror:
I look in the mirror every day,
And see the same reflection
Which never seems to change
Yet the thoughts in my head
Always seem to though
Positive, then negative
And many times I do not even know

I look in the mirror everyday
And tell myself I'll be ok
If I can just ignore those thoughts
I know that I will change a lot
While my heart breathes another
Which one do I listen to?

I look in the mirror everyday
And analyze and stare at what needs to change
For the times when I like what I see
I feel like a different me
The one that I truly am
The one that I know will take a stand
But most of the time that never occurs
I usually feel like a failure, disgusting and unsure

The mirror reflects only an image
For the world around me to see

But that image presently does not portray the real me
One day soon I hope it will
When pointless thoughts will never arise
And confidence will inspire

The beauty on the outside can only be viewed by eyes
While the thought of loving myself lies from deep inside
A mirror will only reflect what the world perceives I am
supposed to be
So I say I throw out the mirrors and work on the real me

While minds will grow
Hearts will love
And one day I'll know
The answer of what I long to be
That will finally reveal the real me

*

Like many of my other journal entries, through expressive writing I was able to tap into things within myself that I really didn't consciously realize affected me. In this poem, it is obvious that I knew the only way to obtain the eternal happiness that I kept searching for this whole time would be accomplished through working from the inside out, rather than the other way around.

I had noticed how the appearance of myself and others around me was just a temporary thing and in time those looks would fade and therefore leave us only with who we remained as on the inside. Yet, like everything else at this time in my life, I was unable to see the value that my own insights carried, as ED was overpowering my life. I didn't trust who I was and what I truly believed and since no one around me was telling me such things like what I wrote, I never used the powerful meanings as a roadmap for finding myself. ED simply continued to control my life.

*

Identity. A lack of one. Don't know who I am. Don't know what I believe. Identity. Needing others to show me who I am. Needing others to define me. Needing others to ensure that I have a self. Am a self. Have a purpose. Identity. Through them. Identity. Now through him.

I was his girlfriend. This is who I was. This was my identity. But now he was gone. Losing what I had with him meant I lost a part of myself. This cycle, this unhealthy cycle that we both kept walking in and out of was ruining both of our lives.

We would still hang out even when we were broken

up, still acting as if we were together even though officially we were not. As a result I, in particular, would damage myself even more by cutting away deeper and deeper at myself when I was alone. I had absolutely no idea how to be alone.

I couldn't handle being alone. I couldn't handle being without him. I didn't know how to be without him, so I turned to ED. ED was always there to replace him. To make me feel whatever Justin was not doing anymore since he was no longer my boyfriend. ED did not have good intentions though. ED was the most manipulative, lying son of a bitch you would ever meet.

Yet, he was also like a chameleon. His perfect words, his countless promises. He always showed up at the right time, whenever I was vulnerable, sad, depressed, and alone. He comforted me by making me my favorite dishes. Telling me that everything would be okay, that I should just focus on losing weight and then things with my ex would turn out the way I wanted them to.

I believed ED. I believed that he was truly going to help me become perfect, which would help me have a perfect relationship again, which would make me perfectly happy, which would make my life perfect. From that first night that I officially met ED, I handed off all of my power over to him; no longer did it remain solely in the hands of my ex-boyfriend, but the other half now belonged to ED. I officially had no control over myself, my actions, my emotions, my being, as it was completely and entirely controlled by others. ED continued to make me focus on my body. On the external. On the fact that I still felt different. I didn't want to feel different anymore. ED had convinced me that my external held all of the answers in finding the happiness that I thought I wanted. Living in the external was completed connected to the shallow. Yet, shallow forms of happiness always lead to breakdowns, as they aren't real. I was currently living inside of this breakdown as ED had taken me as his hostage and was not going to set me free anytime soon.

Unless and until I learned about ED's existence.

These experiences obviously didn't stop happening in my last year of high school. Yet, because the goal of this book is not about sharing my entire life story with you, but rather helping spark some insights into your own experiences that you may have overlooked or thought didn't still affect your life today, I feel that stopping here makes sense.

I hope that from reading some of my personal experiences you have begun to understand why and how ED had created this story around who I saw myself as. As I've mentioned, until I learned about ED's existence, I had no idea that I was walking around with something like an MP3 player within my mind, which kept playing the same fictitious songs to me every day.

The truth was that if you would have told me back then that any of this was going on inside of my mind, I wouldn't have believed you. I was so attached to my thoughts before I learned about ED's existence. All I could focus on was my body. To me my external held all of the answers to find the happiness I wanted. To help me feel like I belonged. The truth was that all of this was just ED's doing. The reason why I would have never believed you if you mentioned this information to me, was because ED was the one who was in control of my life at the time. I had absolutely no idea what an EGO was, or that my thoughts could speak anything other than the truth. This is why I want to share this with all of you, so you can begin to learn about your own EGO, your own ED and figure out what fictitious story he has been playing in your mind day after day.

Another reason why I choose to stop here is that the way in which I continued to live my life from this point onwards was completely and entirely directed by the story of who ED convinced me to believe that I was. I am going to share my story with you again, all tied up nicely in the next paragraph to showcase how all of the experiences that I shared with you before, which left out numerous other experiences and took years to formulate, combined together to create this two paragraph story about "the Paula" that I walked around the world thinking that I was.

My Story

I am imperfect. I need to be fixed. Changed. Altered. I am different and being different is bad. Being different results in people laughing at me. Commenting on my appearance. Making fun of my differences. Standing out is bad. Fitting in is good. Boys only like me because of my breasts. My breasts are way too big and they need to be smaller. Once I lose weight, lose my curves, I will fit in. Until then I am imperfect. Losing weight is my answer and dieting is my means to get there. Unless I am on a diet I won't be a good dancer. Unless I am on a diet, I am not good enough. Unless I am dieting I am wrong. My body must look like my friends. My body must look like a typical dancer's body, therefore not allowed to have curves. My breasts must be smaller than all adults or anyone older than me. I must eat each portion that is outlined to me by a diet at every meal. I must drink a minimum of eight glasses of water a day. I must not eat three hours before I go to bed. I must try to not eat carbs or junk food ever and if I do certainly don't have them for dinner. I must always work out in the morning before I have had anything to eat to burn the most fat. If I don't do these rules, I am wrong, I am bad, I am not perfect. I need to lose weight. I need to be perfect.

I am so fat. I am unlovable. I am dumb. I am ugly. I am not good enough. I need to be perfect. I need to have a perfect body. When I have a perfect body, my boyfriend and I will be back to what we used to be. I need to have my boyfriend in my life. He is the only guy for me. I cannot be alone. I don't know who I am without my friends or my boyfriend. My friends never cared about me. I can never say no. I must always wear a smile on my face and act like everything is fine. I need to lose weight.

Not knowing about my EGO, ED and my story, caused me to treat myself in ways I didn't deserve, allow others to treat me in ways I didn't deserve, miss out on opportunities I really wanted to be a part of and more than anything be controlled by fear. Let me be clear in saying that I do not want this for you.

You probably don't know it right now, but I can guarantee that ED is currently telling you a story about who he thinks you are. Not only has he been telling you this story for years, but he is so good at convincing you to believe that this story is true that you just believe him. This story usually includes things from as far back as when you were five years old. Similarly to mine, as you grew older, this story that ED has been telling you has just gotten longer and longer. This always seems to be a non-fiction story, as ED is very good at presenting it that way. Truth be told, this story is pure fiction. In my opinion, this story serves one purpose: **to keep you stuck exactly where you are.**

Therefore, in order to really live a life free from ED, this story about who you may now *think* you are, is quite essential to recognize.

It is important for me to tell you, that figuring out the story that ED was telling me for years did not happen overnight. Please don't be disappointed or discouraged if you don't know yours right away or if you don't even understand what I am talking about at the moment. That is completely normal, since ED has been dictating your life for so long, he has somewhat become your identity. Learning more about your story will come from a lot of the exercises that you will continue to do in this book, as well as through other exercises that I will suggest you do throughout your day.

If you are feeling unsure about what your story consists of and feel like you need to go back into your past, like I just showed you with a bunch of my past experiences, that's no problem. In the next section, we are going to dive into your past, where as a result of thinking about particular life experiences of yours may help you figure out how the story around who ED has convinced you to believe that you are was formulated. In the next exercise, however, all you need to think about is what are the most common thoughts that you think about in regards to yourself internally, your body, your weight and food. By focusing on the everyday thoughts in regards to these issues you can begin to uncover some of your own story right now.

Remember there is no right or wrong when it comes to this process. The important thing to keep in mind when doing this exercise is that attaining awareness of your internal cognitions and thoughts, which may feel like your own at this time, is the first step in gaining awareness of ED and ultimately learning how to fall in love with yourself, your body and your life.

So now it is your turn to write your own story about the person that ED thinks you are.

(7) Writing The Story About Who ED Thinks You Are

Step One:
I would like you to review all of you answers from the two previous sections where I asked you all of those questions about yourself and your life.

Step Two:
Based on everything you just read about your answers about yourself, your body, your life and your external word, please write the story about who you think you really are, commenting on ANYTHING and EVERYTHING you think you are. (i.e. What type of person do you think you are? Do you think you are smart? Funny? Are you confident? Shy? Pretty? Do you think others like you?)

Once again, please remember there is no right or wrong answer when it comes to writing your story. The more honest and open you can be, the better this exercise will work for you. We will come back to this story later on, so please write it in your journal or put it somewhere special that you'll remember. Lastly, make sure to add the date that you write this story.

Step Three: Write Your Story
Today's Date:_____

_____

_____

_____

_____

_____

_____

_____

_____

_____

_____

_____

_____

_____

_____

_____

_____

_____

_____

_____

_____

_____

_____

_____

I hope by this point of this book you are beginning to understand how your thoughts, which are influenced by ED, affect some of your life choices and opinions. In order to be able to truly fall in love with yourself, your body and your life, having this awareness is essential to begin the next step of truly living a life *separate from ED*. The next section will address just this.

Recap:
Through first gaining awareness of ED I am able to begin to separate from his voice and influence. By learning about the story that ED has been telling me, I am able to further distance myself from him.

I AM AWESOME EXERCISE!

You have now just finished Section A of Part Two of this book!

Before we continue, I want to acknowledge you and tell you that you should be REALLY proud of yourself. You should know the drill right now. Before we move onto the next section I really want you to take this moment to recognize all of the great work you just did again.

Now tell yourself, "I am awesome!" Say it twice more and really believe it!

You may be wondering why I keep asking you to do all of these, "I am awesome" exercises. Well, the reason is because oftentimes in our lives we don't stop along the way towards reaching a goal of ours and acknowledge the amazing work we have done. I feel that learning how to acknowledge ourselves by taking a moment and really recognizing the progress we have made, even if it is a tiny step, is an important part in building our confidence within ourselves and our abilities. You can even take this exercise a step further by rewarding yourself with something you really love (i.e. your favorite latte at a coffee shop, a warm bubble bath, a nice walk by the water or a new journal.) Just make sure you *CHOOSE* something that allows you to acknowledge the steps you have taken towards falling in love with yourself, your body and your life.

August 29.2003
I looked in the mirror. Staring so closely at my face. *My hair is too thin. I have such ugly dark circles. My teeth are so gross.* My eyes worked their way down and stopped at my breasts. *Big. Gross. Wrong. Big. Gross. Wrong.* When I was sick of looking at my breasts, my eyes would trickle down until they hit my stomach. *Used to be nice. Now I am fat. Too wide. Too flabby.* They would go to my hips next. *I wished everything was what it once was when I was younger.* I then stared at my thighs for what felt like hours. *Fat. Huge. Ugly. Enormous. I have the fattest thighs ever. I am so gross. I hate my body. I just hate it.* My eyes would make their way back up to my face. *I am not good enough. I am not smart enough. I am not pretty enough.*

*

No longer is your reflection the way it once was when you were a young child. It has been shaped, malformed and altered into something completely untrue, essentially ED. Yet, when you look at your own reflection, you do not see ED, rather you see the person who you think that you are. A person that is highly influenced, if not entirely directed, by ED's opinions and beliefs which have now become your conditioned thoughts.

When we were young children we were so connected to who we were and knew that our reflection was absolutely perfect just as it was. As we get older no longer is this true, no longer is this the case. Through taking this newfound awareness of EDs existence into our lives we can begin to see him for what he truly is –our EGO. The next section will help you take this awareness of ED and begin to separate yourself from him.

Section B
Establishing Separation from ED

"A person starts to live when he can live outside himself."
–Albert Einstein

Up until now, ED has been trying to convince you that what he has been saying to you is true. He's been the thing that has been dictating and controlling your life. Now that you are starting to question his validity, he may be asking you why or trying to convince you that he knows what he's talking about.

This is all part of the process. ED does not want to lose his power. His goal is always to be wanted. He always wants to be in control. He always feels the need to be attached to something. Now that you are questioning his existence you better believe that he isn't going to just be quiet without a bit of a fight. It is your job to not give up and actively participate in creating a separation from his influence and control. In this next section we will focus on how you can begin to establish separation from ED once and for all and no longer allow him to control your life.

(1) Renaming ED With A Name That Serves You

In establishing a separation from ED it is quite beneficial to give it a name that serves you. As I mentioned at the beginning of part two, you can simply call it ED or EGO, or any name you desire. It doesn't matter what name you choose, just choose one that isn't a name that you feel is your own.

Through choosing a name for your ED, you begin to gain separation from it and learn that it is not essentially you. As you continue to work on gaining awareness of his existence and creating a separation, having a name that is separate from your own will allow the process of falling in love with yourself, your body and your life to be much easier. I am going to continue to refer to it as ED throughout the course of this book.

(2) Exploring EDs Story

In the last section I asked you to write out the story about who you think you really are. I know for some of you that exercise may have been a bit challenging or even extremely difficult. That is completely normal and expected.

Whether or not you were able to write out your story,

I hope at this point of the book you understand that "this story", which I keep referring to, is actually composed of ED's ideas about who he believes you to be.

What this means is this is not necessarily who you *truly* are. Sure, some of what he has been telling you may have resulted in particular behavioral patterns or actions that are somewhat in alignment with what he says and that's completely normal too. The thing that is important to know is that just because you may have acted a certain way in the past, or have done certain things for years, does not mean that those actions, behaviors and choices define who you *truly* are and the person who you yearn to be.

The truth is we each have the power to create the life of our dreams, where our relationship with ourselves and our bodies can all stem from a place of complete and utter love. This is the way we were born into the world, knowing this deep within, a knowledge that showcased itself through a feeling of oneness and connection to everything around us. We knew that we were enough just as we were.

Somewhere along the way this inner wisdom and knowing got lost and replaced by ED. As a result, this state that we are born into is often difficult to reconnect with when ED is controlling our lives and persuading us to engage in behavior that is out of alignment to who we really want to be. We all live in this world that has external pressures, expectations and ideas around who we are meant to be and ED is essentially formulated from that; ED exists off of that.

As for now, all we need to be concerned about and focused on is continuing to gain the awareness that ED even exists, because it is through this awareness that we are able to begin to shift, that we are able to make different choices, and more than anything, that our *true* selves have an opportunity to show up even momentarily and be at the forefront.

You may be thinking, *"Well if these opinions toward and about myself are only ED's and not actually my own, how do I know who I really am?"* Well the first step in doing this is going back to the story that ED has been telling you for years and recognizing that on some level it feels completely true to you.

I know for myself, when I started going through this process and I would go back to my own story, there was always this part of me that believed that "this story" was who I really was. Looking back, it was as if I was an actress playing the part of "this Paula" in the story that ED had written for me. Yet, because I had no idea that there was even a role I was playing in a story written by ED, I just assumed the way I thought, acted and behaved solely represented who I truly was.

I completely ignored the fact that when I was a little girl I was connected to the truth and was completely and blissfully happy with who I was. When I was an innocent child, where authentic self-expression, self-love and freedom embodied my way of being, I thought that this feeling was just naïvete or even ignorance, rather than a connection to something completely authentic, real and true. We use so many common phrases like, *"well they are just kids, they don't know anything"*, it's almost as if it made me believe that anything that felt like real and utter joy as a child had some sort of expiry date associated to it.

Ultimately, this way of thinking is just another reflection of the power that ED plays in everybody's mind. ED does not acknowledge this, but rather disregards it completely by labeling children as unaware. Sure they may not be educated in the way in which our world is set up, but they have something that most adults do not have – a connection to their real selves. They say what they want without fear or worry and they listen to their body by telling you when they are hungry or full.

I remember sitting in the mall once and this five year

old girl walked by me, stopped dead in her tracks and started waving to me. Her parents continued walking forward, not realizing that she had stop to say hello to me. I thought this was absolutely adorable and had a quick conversation with this little girl. I could feel and sense her connection to this authentic and true place that we all as human beings have.

Yet, if an adult did the same thing to me this experience would not be interpreted in the same manner.

This kind of behavior is deemed as being socially inappropriate and could get misinterpreted as something even worse. But why? Why is it inappropriate or seen as odd for a complete stranger to stop at the mall and say hello to you if they feel so inclined to do so?

It's through social conditioning. That little girl who acted on impulse, who showcased the connection to her truth without the interference of ED will one day no longer stop in the mall and wave hello to whomever she feels the desire to, because ED will take over, as he does for all of us. I do not believe this to be good or bad — it's just what happens.

However, through gaining awareness that this takes place we can begin to see the way in which social conditioning plays such an enormous role in the way in which we act, think and live.

Going back to my earlier point that within ED's story there lies instances that whether or not they are factual, on some level feel real to you. For example, if part of your story is that, *"You are stupid and not good enough,"* I can guarantee you that there is at least one circumstance that happened in your life that made you feel that *"You are stupid and not good enough,"* is actually true.

With this understanding in mind, I would like you to go back to that page in your journal where you wrote out your story and answer the questions I have outlined below.

Before you begin, it is important to note that there may be many layers involved within the story that you have written about yourself. For example, in my personal story some of the things I believed about myself was that, *"I am fat, I am not good enough, I need to be perfect, and dieting holds all of my answers."* Even though each thought was somewhat connected to the others, each belief still held individual value and meaning on its own. I am telling you this, so you can use it as an example for yourself when you are answering the following questions. To get the most out of the questions below, I suggest that you break down your story thought by thought, belief by belief, in order to really be able to address each part on its own. For those of you who had a difficult time writing out your story in the last section, that is no problem; work with what you have. If you haven't written anything then I suggest that you move onto the next section, which may actually help you uncover your story.

Questions About Your Story

(1) Is there actual truth in each point of the story that you wrote about yourself? If so, why do you believe that it is true? How do you know that it is true?

(2) If you believe that these points are all made up and your story is not true, when do you believe that story began in your life?

(3) Was there a particular instance(s) that caused this thought/belief to show-up?

(4) Do you remember when you first started thinking these thoughts? Were you in school? Were you a young child? A pre-teen? A teenager? An adult?

(5) Is what you wrote about in your story something that you have been thinking about for years? Can you remember when it first started?

(6) I would like you to prove how the thought/belief that you have written is actually true in

your eyes? What facts do you have from your life to prove that this belief is true? For example:

- If you are saying that you are not very smart, do you have a job? Are you or have your been in school? You were smart enough to buy this book and read it up until this point, so how are you not smart?

- If you wrote that you are fat, but you know that your actual weight is not considered overweight for your height, then when did this "story" become real to you? If you are overweight for your height, have you always been? If not, when did you put on the weight? Do you have any idea as to why you put the weight on? Is it something that you are concerned about and would like to change? Why or why not? If you have always been overweight why do you feel that you have been? Is it something that you are concerned about and would like to change? Why or why not?

- If you wrote that you are not good enough, in what aspect of your life did this feeling of not being good enough show up? When did this feeling come up for you? How in your eyes is it true?

- If you wrote that, skinnier people are smarter, more accomplished and successful, who told you that? Can you name some individuals who are not necessarily skinny who are smart, accomplished and successful?

I am asking you these very important questions because oftentimes we become so accustomed to simply believing in exactly what ED says to us. Yet, through breaking down his story about us and questioning each of his ideas about who he has convinced us to think that we are and trying to prove them wrong, we can find that there is really no accuracy in his ideas about us. Rather, his ideas are fabrications of the truth based on particular instances that have happened in our lives, which he has misinterpreted.

In the excerpts that I shared with you about my past, you were able to read about some experiences that I went through while I was growing up. For example, when I was ten years old, I was unable to take a step back and understand that as a preteen going through puberty earlier than most of the girls in my grade, boys would obviously make comments about my appearance. I was too attached to those instances that made me feel bad about myself and internalized them to believe that there was not only something wrong with my appearance, but that there was something wrong with who I was.

This in fact was all the workings of ED, because the truth was that the real me, the one I was as an infant, knows that this is absolutely false. The real me knows that I am enough just as I am, just like the real you knows this about you. Yet, when ED shows up and misinterprets events that happen to us, through taking everything personally and adding meaning to each experience that occurs, he causes us to disconnect further and further from this part of ourselves.

The goal in this is not to beat yourself up or be mad at yourself for walking around with this fictional idea about who you are based on experiences you encountered. Rather, it is to gain some insight and understanding into the fact that you did interpret these experiences to hold the absolute truth, when in reality it was just an experience that eventually passed.

In our minds these traumatic and often life altering experiences do not just pass when they are over, they remain inside of the walls of our minds being held captive by ED who continues to replay them over and over and over again until they essentially malform into the story of who we believe we are. It is important to remember that ED is founded in fear and all of his stories and interpretations of things are founded in fear.

If you think of it this way, you can begin to see the story that has been playing in your mind like that MP3 player I spoke about earlier. When thinking about your relationship to your body, yourself and your weight, you can picture this MP3 player automatically and continuously playing fictional songs about the way you *should* look, what foods you *should* and *shouldn't* eat and the way you *should* feel about yourself. These songs are essentially a part of your story.

I acknowledge that you may be a bit confused right now. This way of thinking is certainly different than most people are used to, especially when ED is controlling our thoughts and we are unaware of his existence. Once, again this is completely normal and expected. I promise you though as you work through the material in this book, this will all start to make more sense. As for now, it may be important to take another look at the stories that ED tells you daily.

As we learned about in the last section these stories are formulated as a result of your past. These stories can be filled with things you *can* or *cannot do,* what you *should* and *shouldn't do,* what you are *capable of* and *what you are not capable of, what your body should look like* and *what it shouldn't* and more. Oftentimes our stories are filled with restrictions, limitations and negative ideas about the type of person we are so convinced we not only have to be, but can only be. The truth is we can be and do anything that we want.

Before we move onto the next section, I would like to ask you a few questions.

Are you committed to letting go of this story and moving forward from it? Do you want to learn how to let this story that has been playing in your mind for years like a never ending song, no longer control your actions, behaviors and way you feel about yourself? Are you interested in learning what your life would be like if this story no longer existed and did not hold your identity and defined who you think you are anymore?

If you answered no, then I would like you to journal around why you are feeling resistance towards moving forward with your life and actually learning how to fall in love with yourself, your body and your life.

I know oftentimes it can be scary to move forward into a place of the unknown. Yet, to me it is much scarier to become stuck inside of a place and way of being that clearly isn't serving you. Oftentimes it feels easier just to stay where we are right now. I remember that feeling of resistance whenever I was moving outside of my comfort zone and was essentially walking into unknown territory. The thing that I always asked myself that usually helped me move forward whenever I felt stuck, which I suggest you ask yourself now, is ***Is it more comfortable to stay inside of the world I am currently living in now, one that is controlled by ED, filled with fear and is comfortably uncomfortable or is it worth the shot of trying to move forward past this block and just let go and trust in the process? Even though I don't know what is going to happen once I move forward, can I just begin to trust that this feeling of resistance and fear that I am having is occurring for a reason, to try to teach me something about myself and my life and believe that whatever comes as a result is meant to?***

What's holding you back from saying yes?

- If you find that you are stuck, I suggest you contact me at www.paulagalli.com and I can help you uncover what is blocking you from wanting to move forward.

If you answered yes to the question, then the next section of this book will allow you to do just that.

You now may begin to realize the enormous power

that your story has been playing in your life. Even though you can see this, it doesn't automatically mean that everything is going to shift and you are just going to be able to live your life as your *true* self, completely separate from ED today, tomorrow, next week or even next month. In order to answer a lot of the questions I just asked you, I find that going into the past is not only highly important, but essential. In this next section you are going to begin to understand why trying to move forward in creating a life without ED controlling you is impossible unless and until you clean up your past.

Recap:
The story that I have been telling myself for years, the one which I have identified myself to who I believe I really am, is actually ED. Through beginning to hear ED's story and questioning its truth, I can begin to see how this is not actually me, but rather an idea of who I thought I was.

(3) The Importance of Learning How To Clean Up Your Past

Where did everything that we have spoken about up until now in regards to ED's influences that affected your current thoughts and beliefs of yourself occur? - IN THE PAST!

If you really think about it, a lot of the things that ED says to you every day and the way in which you see the world are influenced by things that happened to you in your past. Hopefully, my examples showcase this point; it was through my experiences that ED formulated the story of who I thought I was. If I did not become aware of ED's existence I would still be walking around playing that story within my mind daily, believing it was me. I am so happy that I am aware of his existence and no longer allow past experiences to define who I am. My intention is for you to feel the same, yet until you learn about your own story it is impossible to no longer be defined by it.

As we spoke about earlier, ED has created stories about the way things *should be, ought to be, need to be* and *need not to be*. We see life and, furthermore, ourselves through a filter that is conditioned and altered as a result of ED's beliefs created from our past. In order to really begin to separate from ED's voice and power I feel that it is extremely important to clean up the past.

Depending on what your past looks like you may have a lot of messes to clean up or very few. Some of these messes include and involve other people, particular situations, or simply the way in which you have treated yourself. Regardless of what has happened to you in your past, it is essential to take the necessary steps to deal with, heal and gain closure over these instances that often keep you stuck from moving forward in the manner you would really like to.

You may be asking yourself, *"So how do I do this?"*

Well, in order to create and live the life that you have always wanted to have for yourself, oftentimes going into the past is essential. Numerous programs and particular coaches may disagree with what I am saying, but in my professional and personal opinion I feel that it is almost impossible to truly transform yourself and your life into what and who you have always wanted to be if there are younger versions of yourself that are still experiencing pain.

Sure you today at whatever age you are may not be feeling any pain in regards to what happened to you when you were let's say, eight years old, but that doesn't mean that the eight year old does not still exist inside of you. This eight year old who resides inside of you still feels incomplete about a particular instance that happened in your past. Your current self may be unable to sustain any of the life goals that you have wanted to accomplish for yourself; this inner child's desire to not only be heard and recognized, but most importantly consoled about the issues and pain that they experienced, may be linked to why you find it difficult to implement and sustain any real changes that you have wanted.

For example, I was working with a client who'd been living with a pretty severe Eating Disorder since she was twelve years old. At that age, her life felt very out of control due to the fact that her mother was in and out of the hospital for her own Eating Disorder. Twenty years later, she was sitting in my office telling me about her daily episodes of binging and purging and how to her this was just a normal way of being. She had been doing this since she was twelve years old. It had become a daily habit that she had formed.

I first tried to talk to her about her binging and purging episodes as something that she was engaging in as a thirty-two year old woman only and how we could set up different ways for her to try to stop this behavior, but this seemed to only get us so far. She logically understood everything that I was saying and agreed. Yet, week after week, nothing really changed.

I finally approached this from the place of connecting with her twelve year old self as well, for this was the part of her that initially began engaging in this behavior, not as a means of habit but from a place of coping with what she was going through at that time. Though I still acknowledged that binging and purging was a coping mechanism for her today, the way I believed that she would truly break free from this behavior was through ensuring that not only did her current self receive the healing and closure she needed, but that this twelve year old girl did as well.

I asked her to explain to me what was going on in this time of her life that made her feel like binging and purging was the only answer. I asked her to describe to me what she felt like during these years. Essentially the goal of this was to get her to begin to reconnect with that younger girl inside of her. To allow her to speak up and to express what she was experiencing during that time. This was highly important for her process moving forward because this twelve year old girl inside of her never was able to truly express her feelings about the reality that she was living in.

Even if you have never experienced an Eating Disorder at all, or on this part of the spectrum, it is important to note that when you are trying to change any relationships in your life, especially when it comes to the relationship that you have with your body, eating and food, going back into the past and beginning to uncover and clean up whatever ideas you initially formulated around these issues back then is often more beneficial than just simply trying to feel motivation to stick to a new diet plan, exercise regimen or any other type of restrictive behavioral changes.

Remember, my goal is to guide you to fall in love with yourself, your body and your life, **for the rest of your life**, not just for the next month!

In the excerpts that I shared with you about my past, you can see that there are multiple instances at different ages where I encountered experiences that were never even acknowledged as instances that deeply affected me. Since I was unaware that these encounters really affected me, I shoved them under the rug, pushing them down deep and acting as if they no longer bothered me. Yet, as I grew older and new experiences which also deeply affected me were taking place, I not only tried to ignore those current experiences, but was also walking around with younger versions of myself experiencing pain from the past as well.

With this all being said, who is to say that there isn't also a four year old, twelve year old and seventeen year old inside of you who are still feeling incomplete about something that happened to them? Did you, like me, just push those experiences deep down and "get over them" by ignoring that they had taken place? Is your younger self trying to communicate with you about something but you just don't listen?

If you have never revisited your past, I can guarantee that this is taking place because the truth is we all have younger versions of ourselves that reside inside of us and communicate with us from time to time. If any emotional and/or traumatic experiences happened during our past and there was no closure or healing around these instances, letting go and moving forward in creating a life you truly love living is often-times impossible.

Yet, most people continue to disconnect from these parts of themselves and their past in the belief that if they ignore it or shove it under the rug and solely focus on becoming this new person and creating the life they really want, that it will just happen. They may feel that there is really no need to go back into the past, revisit past emotions or experiences because they are "over it." Just like with my client's example, she logically understood that she was unable to deal with her mother being in and out of the hospital so she turned to this type of behavior as a coping mecha-nism to deal with it. However even with this under-standing today it didn't mean that the twelve year old girl inside of her understood this, for it is the twelve year old girl inside of her that needed to be heard and spoken to. As I mentioned above, sure the you today may be over it but that doesn't mean that the eight year old is. Sure you logically can understand what happened to you when you were eight and don't find it that big of a deal anymore, but does the eight year old inside of you? Did the eight year old get spoken to, consoled and told that everything will be okay? Likely not.

This is exactly what I am speaking about. I believe that this is the BIG missing piece of the puzzle, the key ingredient in not only creating the life of your dreams but sustaining it. Without it, even when we get inspired to make any changes in our life, more often than not, these changes slowly fade away and old thought patterns and behaviors revisit. Why? Is it because you are not motivated and just lazy? No, not at all. Is it because you are not capable of actually following through with what you want to do for yourself, your body and your life? Nope, not even close. Even though there are a number of reasons that ED will tell you why you "failed", I want you to know that those are not the *real* reasons. The *real* reason why these behavioral changes are not actually taking place and sticking in your life is because of two things.

(1) Circumstances in your past that haven't been truly healed and received the closure they needed to be laid to rest – therefore, inner

child work is needed

(2) Your thoughts are not in alignment to what you are currently trying to bring and attract into your life – therefore, we need to change, alter and select your thoughts

In this particular section of the book we are going to be focusing on the first reason – inner child work. Later on we will address the second reason.

(A) Healing The Past

In the paragraph above I mentioned the concept of healing around those issues. When I talk about cleaning up the past another way to look at it is to heal the past. As you begin to gain awareness into why you may currently act a certain way or why you may have made particular life choices in the past, that awareness and understanding does not necessarily bring closure and healing to those instances. All the awareness does is allow you to gain the ability to recognize and see that this experience has happened to you. Furthermore, this awareness also allows you to see the thoughts that ED is constantly saying to you and to begin to become detached from those thoughts.

As a result, you begin to step into the ***role of the observer of your thoughts*** versus ***being auto-***

matically reactive, responsive and controlled by what ED says.

Furthermore, in the role of the observer you begin to **develop the ability to see your thoughts and emotions** and then **CHOOSE how to act,** as opposed to just being and acting on automatic.

It is through this power of CHOICE that real freedom lies. I say this because when you begin to learn that you have the power of CHOOSING what to think and how to act, you literally have the ability to CHOOSE your life. I will address this concept of CHOICE later on in the book as well. As for now all you need to know is that even though I feel that having awareness of ED and his thoughts, is one of the first steps in learning how to truly fall in love with yourself, your body and your life, as I just mentioned, having this awareness does not necessarily bring healing or closure to those instances.

You may be asking yourself, *"So how do I do bring healing or closure to those instances?"*

Well, you can think about it this way, all of the instances in your past that you may feel emotionally connected to are still emotionally triggering you for a reason. If they didn't affect you anymore they wouldn't stir up such powerful emotions and feelings.

To make this easier, you can think about these emotional triggers or feelings as if they are scars on your body. Each of these scars are covered by a bandage; a bandage that has been on you since you initially decided to move forward from this painful experience and not heal it. Please, please do not judge that you may be wearing lots of bandages right now, as this way of being is very typical behavior in our society. We are told to *get over things, let it go, move on, be strong, find someone new, pull up our socks, not to take it personally* and so on and so forth. We are always geared towards moving away from our uncomfortable feelings because on some level we believe that's what we *should* be doing.

There are so many external stimuli provided to us in our society that allow us to escape those uncomfortable feelings such as food, booze, drugs, television, games, exercise, gambling, shopping and more. Again, the intention of presenting this idea to you is not to cause you to place any blame on yourself if you participate in any of these escapist behaviors. The truth is as humans, we all do it sometimes in one form or another. I certainly am no exception to this. However, when I turn to any external stimuli as a sporadic coping mechanism now, I am completely aware of the fact when I am doing it, compared to when I used to automatically turn to these means without feeling like I had a choice in the matter. Problems can arise when we turn to these stimuli as a daily coping mechanism. By gaining the awareness of our behavior, we may begin to receive insight as to why we do what we do and, furthermore, begin to ask ourselves the questions as to why those have become our automatic behavioral responses. Those automatic responses are simply just another indication that ED is at work, as his goal is to essentially "protect us" and keep us "safe." Yet, ED's interpretation for keeping us safe and protecting us is situated in fear. He associates discomfort with harm when oftentimes uncomfortable feelings are anything except harmful, they are ways we can begin to connect with our true selves, can experience growth and can gain closure and healing. All you need to know is that the whole intention behind me asking you to revisit your past is to allow those bandages to come off once and for all because they are no longer needed. They will no longer be needed if the scar, sprain, cut, bump or bruise that they have been protecting is finally healed.

I believe that by revisiting the past and taking the necessary steps to allow our younger selves to first be heard and consoled for what they are feeling and secondly, to have somebody who loves them very much tell them everything you wish you heard at that moment in time, is truly necessary. By creating an alternative ending to those particular instances or circumstances where your younger self is left in a much more happy, complete, understanding, consoled, heard and healed environment, you have now closed the past in a different way than it has been dealt with up until now.

Before we continue I would like to ask you a question: Is receiving closure and healing of your past something that you would like to do?

If your answer is no, I invite you to journal as to what is blocking you from wanting to receive closure and healing of your past. I suggest that you go back to the original intention that you first wrote about why you picked up this book to begin with, as this may remind you why you are doing this exercise.

If you are unable to get to the place where you feel the desire to want to heal your past, I invite you to contact me at www.paulagalli.com or find a local therapist who can help you sort out this reasoning.

If your answer is yes, there are a few things you need to know in order to experience this complete closure of your past.

(1) The Healing Crisis: Things Sometimes Get Worse Before They Get Better

Sometimes things have to get worse before they get better. The concept of the Healing Crisis explains this perfectly. A Healing Crisis often happens when a person is undergoing some sort of natural therapy usually associated with healing their physical body. When individuals begin to heal, without warning, they can re-experience the physical symptoms that may have disappeared for a while. This oftentimes results in people feeling upset or discouraged, leaving them to think that the process isn't working since their old symptoms have resurfaced. This is the time where many people will give up on the healing process and convince themselves that whatever they were doing wasn't working.

In actuality, what they are experiencing is simply a healing crisis. When healing takes place, the body may reintroduce painful symptoms as a means of releasing toxins. This is actually a great sign that the healing is taking place within the body; it is eliminating everything it no longer needs and beginning to heal itself in the process. In the context of this book, I think that the Healing Crisis can also occur in regards to healing our mental and emotional lives as well.

By going into the past we may uncover old painful wounds that we have tried to suppress for many years. Through the exercises I am going to walk you through in this book, which will cause you to go back into your past and in turn allow a lot of potentially painful and uncomfortable memories to resurface, you may begin to feel as though you are somewhat going backwards with the ways in which you respond to these feelings. You may be feeling quite great about yourself thus far through all of the personal work that you have been doing. Yet, the truth is just like with our physical bodies that experience a Healing Crisis where which the body allows the symptoms to resurface as a means of releasing everything it no longer needs, the same can be said about the mental/emotional process as well. By revisiting past memories with the intention of healing them, the body may experience painful and uncomfortable emotions, mental thought process and physical sensations or pain as a means of healing that emotional wound. Just like with the physical body, this experience of resurfaced pain or discomfort is actually part of the healing process itself.

I know this not only personally but professionally as well. I have not worked with any clients who haven't told me after a couple of weeks or months that they feel like they are moving backwards. As we begin to uncover their past, painful experiences resurface, causing uncomfortable feelings to show up. This often results in them returning to old behaviors and thought patterns and/or turn to external stimuli as a means of coping with what they have uncovered.

For the females that I have worked with who have an ED that is also an Eating Disorder, when they find themselves engaging in old behaviors with food and their bodies, that they were trying to change and of-tentimes had changed for months even, in their minds this meant that they had just gone backwards and failed. I let them know that this was completely and utterly false, as it made sense that these new exposed wounds filled with uncomfortable feelings would cause them to engage in old actions, thought patterns and behaviors that at one time were their means of coping and survival, essentially ED's doing.

I also told them that it was important to know that in the process of healing and ultimately transforming a past painful experience, the road to recovery is not a straight and narrow pathway, but rather a twisted road that can often confuse us and make us feel lost.

I wanted to share this with you because oftentimes when we are doing this type of work we want to give up or quit when things get tough, hard, and uncom-fortable or we feel like we have failed because we engaged in old behaviors and we interpret that as a sign that nothing is happening, working or going to change.

Engaging in these old behaviors and coping mechanism is not an indication that you have gotten off track or that nothing is ever going to permanently change. Rather, it is an opportunity for you to use your newfound awareness of ED's existence and CHOOSE to cope with these exposed wounds in a different way.

Due to the fact that we are going to be ripping off bandages that have been covering up scars, it would make complete sense that there may be a bit of discomfort or uncomfortable feelings that occur as a result of that bandage being removed. Allowing yourself to feel those feelings that resurface is one of the key steps in letting them heal. It is in this exact moment that real and substantial healing is actually taking place. It is simply our job to just ride the waves and stick it out because these feelings shall pass, as the healing occurs. Journaling about what is going on throughout this process is a great way to help these feelings pass through us, as well. Essentially, learning how to let go and begin to trust in this healing process as well as having compassion, patience, forgiveness and understanding towards yourself during this time is highly important.

I do completely acknowledge that this is a lot easier said than done. The clients of mine who have an ED that is also an Eating Disorder are often unable to sit with these uncomfortable feelings I speak of. These uncomfortable feelings may surface as anxiety, depression, guilt, resentment, hate, revenge, anger, worry or shame and they are unsure of how to process and just be with them. As a result, ED shows up as a means of, once again, disconnecting them from the truth of what is going on; that they are experiencing uncomfortable feelings that they are unsure of how to just sit with. ED causes them to engage in behaviors and develop thought patterns that are highly connected and focused on their body and food as a means to escape these feelings.

I know this first hand, as I lived this way for years. I was so unable to connect with these uncomfortable feelings, I almost felt that if I sat with them I was going to die or explode. I could not understand them, process them or acknowledge that they were simply just feelings that human beings were meant to feel. I had no idea that once I learned how to just let go and surrender into these feelings that they would eventually pass. As a result, ED showed up for me as means to escape these emotions and essentially try to control and manage everything around me in hopes that if I had everything perfectly controlled and planned out that I would never have to experience those emotions again. That if I ate perfectly and had the perfect body that I would be perfectly happy and as a result these uncomfortable feelings that I hated more than anything would never return.

This way of being is not how we are meant to live. We are not meant to be living through our EDs, trying to control and manipulate everything exactly how we think it should be in order to try to avoid uncomfortable feelings that may surface. We are not meant to shove things under the rug and move forward without cleaning them up. We are not meant to be disconnected from our truth, the truth that often is trying to speak to us through these uncomfortable feelings that we are so terrified of facing.

Yet, if we begin to go back into the past with the intention of healing it, we can have a reminder as to why these uncomfortable feelings that resurface are actually a good thing. They are a sign that we are no longer completely disconnected but are beginning to connect with ourselves and separate from ED once again. We can begin to see that we are not only beginning to actually heal our past but also allowing ourselves to connect with it.

In order to receive some clarity and understanding around the feelings that may come up along the way, answering the following questions may be quite helpful. I suggest that you use your journal as a means to express these answers if you like.

(1) Where are those feelings in your body? (i.e. Stomach, chest, lower abdominal, shoulders)
(2) What do these feelings feel like? (i.e. Sharp pain, aches, knots, stiffness)
(3) What do these feelings make you feel like doing when you feel them? (i.e. Eat, not eat, drink, call a friend, go work out, journal, sleep, bring your hands to the place where the pain subsides, cry, have a cigarette)

Another thing that may result during this Healing Crisis, something that I highly encourage you to do, is to cry. Just like we briefly talked about before, our society puts out a lot of messages as to what and who we *should* or *shouldn't* be like. Terms and common phrases such as, "big girls don't cry", or "boys don't cry" or "crying means your weak", or "don't cry because you *should* be able to hold it together", or "don't cry because you *should* be strong" are simply just another indication and representation of ED being at play. You can begin to recognize this for yourself by asking yourself the following questions,

- Who made up this "rule" about how I should act?
- Who made up this "rule" about who I should be?
- Who made up this "rule" about what crying means?
- Do I want to continue to live my life according to these "rules"?

I tell clients this all of the time. When we are born there is no tag attached to our foot indicating who we have to be. We have learned now that it is through our families, our friends, our generation, the media, religion, our society's and our culture's influences that ED begins to formulate certain thoughts and ideas around what we *should* be and how we *should* act. Bottom line, anytime you hear yourself think or say the word *should*, it is a red flag to dig deeper and really ask yourself why you believe this. Is it what you really believe or what ED has convinced you to believe is true?

Oftentimes people respond by saying, "Well this is how I always have been, or it *should* be this way because that's how it's *supposed* to be." If thoughts such as these have come up for you, I have a few questions to ask you before we continue.

(1) I understand that you have always been this way. Is being that way serving you? Why or why not?

(2) How has being and thinking this way been working out for you? How has being and thinking this way not been working out for you?

(3) Who decided that it was supposed to be this way and why does what they say necessarily feel right to you?

(4) What would it feel like if you were living a life where you CHOOSE to act a particular way that had no *shoulds, have tos* and *needs to bes* involved?

I would like you to think of this process of going into the past in such a way, as if your entire body was composed of broken bones. If you were covered from head to toe with broken bones, would you have the expectation that you would be able to live your life in the exact same manner that you were living it as when your bones were not broken? Would you get upset at yourself when someone asked you to go for a run and you had to say no? Would you judge yourself when you cried from the pain that your body was enduring from all of those bones being broken?

Of course not. You would simply understand that you

needed to allow your body to rest and heal. As a result, you needed to be patient, compassionate, understanding and forgiving of how you may act in the meantime since you are in a lot of pain and are experiencing disappointment because your life isn't exactly how you wished it was at that particular moment.

Having this example in mind, I want to ask you to take this same mentality wherein patience, understanding, forgiveness and compassion are at the forefront of your mind and approach the process of cleaning up your past in the same manner.

Having this level of compassion for yourself will allow the healing process to occur much more smoothly.

Lastly, when we are going into the past and healing a lot of our emotional and mental wounds, we may experience a lot of exhaustion. Just as we would understand being tired as a result of knowing that the physical body would be working on overload to repair all of the broken bones, we need to understand and see that healing our emotional and mental selves is also a highly taxing process on our bodies. I say this for anyone who notices that they are feeling tired or drained as a result of this process. Even though you may feel like you have no reason to be tired, I want to assure you that you do! I would encourage you to allow yourself to have as much downtime as you can during this process. Sleep when you feel you need to, watch movies, take bubble baths or do whatever you can to take care of yourself as you begin to take off the bandages and start to heal your wounds. It is also through this process of downtime, reflection, relaxation and truly taking care of yourself that the healing will take place.

At this point you have the understanding that a Healing Crisis, where things may get worse before they get better, is not only expected but is actually a key part of the healing process. There is one more thing that you need to know in order to experience complete closure of your past. The next section will address this.

(2) How ED Can Cause Us To Play the Role of the Victim

It is important to note that when we go into the past we oftentimes will bring up memories or instances that are highly affected by other people and that involve other people. As children, we do not always have the understanding that others, just like ourselves, are going through their own process and journey of life, where they are learning their own lessons and trying to figure it all out.

We oftentimes tend to take things very personally. We

can begin to take things to heart and as a result make everything about us, when in actuality many situations that we may be a part of might have absolutely nothing to do with us.

For example, if two friends are in a fight and you are there, you may feel it is your responsibility to try to fix everything between your friends, when in actuality the situation has nothing to do with you. Another example is when children feel that it is their responsibility or fault that their parents may have gotten a divorce. In reality, the reason their parents got divorced had nothing to do with them and everything to do with the dynamic of the parents' relationship. This particular way of thinking, where everything involves *me* or *it's always my fault*, or *it is my responsibility to fix things*, or thinking that when someone is in a bad mood *it is because of me*, is a perfect representation that ED is standing at the forefront of our thoughts. ED has a way of making everything about him, therefore, making you feel that everything is about you.

On the other side of the spectrum, we can go into the past and re-experience emotions where we feel we were dealt a wrong hand, a broken heart, were ridiculed, hurt, judged or disempowered because of someone else. In this case you no longer see life as a result of your own choices and behaviors, but actually as the outcome of what someone else did to you. You start thinking things such as, *he did this to me so that is why I can't do this*, or *it is her fault that I am this way*, or *it is my boss that makes me so angry*, or *it is my parents' fault I am like this*. Behaving in this manner and thinking in this particular mindset where you avoid all responsibility for your own life is also another perfect representation of ED.

It's really important to remember that you will never have the ability to change other people.
You will never have control over their behaviors, actions, thought processes or interactions.
What you do and always have had control over is yourself.

I feel a bit hesitant to use the word control because when you are living a life with an ED who is also an Eating Disorder, control is a very big part of him showing up in the first place. Eating Disorders are highly connected to the feeling of needing to have control over everything in life. This usually stems from a lack of trust, something I have mentioned a few times in this book now. Not only trust of oneself, but trust in the process of life. As a result of this lack of trust, individuals with Eating Disorders often feel the need to try to control what they eat, the number on the scale, the numbers of calories burned or the size of their pants.

Alternatively, Eating Disorders oftentimes result when a person feels that their life is so out of control that it is embodied by the lack of control they feel they have around what they eat, the number on the scale, the numbers of calories burned or the size of their pants. If you are someone who is living with an ED that is also an Eating Disorder you will know exactly what I mean by what I just said.

Regardless whether your ED represents an Eating Disorder or not, when I say the term *control* in this particular context I am speaking about the fact that you do not have the direct power to make someone do what you want them to do. You do, however, have direct power over yourself. This direct power is connected to your ability to *CHOOSE* not to listen to ED and make *CHOICES* in your decision making, behaviors, actions and thought processes that you truly are proud of.

If something isn't working for you and your life, you do have the power to change it. Yet, when we are living with ED he will oftentimes keep you living inside of victim mode by making the kind of statements I mention above such as, *"That person did this to me, so I can't do that"* or *"If only I had this, then I could be happy"* and so forth.

No matter what excuses ED feeds you, you do have the *CHOICE* to allow ED to control you and run your life or not. You have the *CHOICE* to live your life as a powerless victim. I know this may sound harsh, but let me be clear that is not my intention. I am not here to make you feel bad or place judgment on you. However, I am here to help encourage you to see ED for who he is and the way in which listening to him is causing the results that you're currently experiencing in your life.

I am also here to try to help teach you about ED's way, and how he oftentimes places blame, judgment, or criticism upon others in order to avoid taking any real responsibility. This in turn results in giving you the opportunity to hear ED through all of the awareness exercises that you have been doing thus far and in turn *CHOOSING* to take responsibility for your own life, regardless of what he may say.

From personal experience I know what it feels like to walk around the world feeling sorry for myself, placing the blame as to why I was the way I was on others and ultimately allowing ED to use the victim card as the ruler of my life. I would say and think things such as, *"You don't understand what I went through"* or *"You cannot relate because no one has ever done this to you."* Rather than acknowledge that I had the *CHOICE* to think a different way, that I had the *CHOICE* to go to therapy and try to deal with my issues, that I had the *CHOICE* to no longer interact with those people who were not a good influence for me, I automatically listened to ED. Again, I did so because I had no idea of his existence, but the thing is you are aware now, so there is no longer an excuse as to why you cannot begin to *CHOOSE* an option that better serves your life and supports your overall intention.

I feel that this is the perfect opportunity for me to talk about something that can happen when we start to bring not only the awareness, but the separation, of ED in our lives. Trying to use this newfound knowledge of ED's existence and enormous influence in our lives does not allow his awareness to be used as a scapegoat.

What I mean by this is oftentimes when we begin to learn about ED's existence we may say things like, *"Well that's not me who is thinking or acting that way, that is just ED."* Though it is great that you are beginning to see the separation of yourself from ED, we don't want to get into the space of avoiding responsibility for our actions and behaviors because we believe that it is ED who was controlling us. Though

ED may be the one who is making us think a certain way, or may try to persuade us to engage in particular behaviors, it doesn't negate the fact that we are still responsible for our own *CHOICES*. There was a time in my life where I was saying these exact same things like, *"Oh that's not me, it's just ED,"* and on some level, I tried to avoid responsibility for my actions. Sure, ED could have been the one in control at the moment, but at the end of the day I still had the *CHOICE* to ask for help, to share what was going on, to listen and not act and to ultimately have direct power over myself.

Though it is important to note that even though you may be beginning to step into the role of the observer of your thoughts and of ED, it doesn't mean that he won't still be highly influential in your decisions and behaviors. I wanted to share this with you because I believe that having this knowledge is quite powerful, especially before we step into the past and try to clean it up the best way we are able.

This knowledge allows you to have realistic expectations of what the process of separation from ED looks like. It also allows you to take full responsibility for your own life and actions. Hopefully it also makes you be more compassionate, forgiving, patient, understanding and loving with yourself when you find that ED is still around and controlling your actions and behaviors. If we can remember that we always have the power of *CHOICE*, we can begin to see our relationships with ourselves, our bodies and our lives from a different standpoint.

Now that you are aware of the things that may come up as a result of you going back into your past, it is time to get into the exercises.

Recap:
In order to truly begin to fall in love with yourself, your body and your life, cleaning up your past is essential. It is important to note that a Healing Crisis may occur when you begin to start this process where things may seem to get worse before they get better. It is also important to be aware of what ED may say to you when you step into the past. He oftentimes tries to keep you stuck by taking things entirely personally and causing you to play the victim card by putting the blame on other people's shoulders. Regardless of what ED may say, you always have the direct power over yourself and your *CHOICES*.

(4) Exercises For Cleaning Up Your Past

For a lot of people, going back to the past and reopening closed wounds is more frightening than the thought of having a root canal with no anesthesia.

Even though we can often get so good at dealing with what has happened to us in our lives through consciously understanding why things have happened, or putting all of that under a rug, behind a closet, or locked away behind unhealthy behaviors such as disordered eating, drinking, drugs, gambling, shopping, overworking, over exercising, watching TV or more, it doesn't mean that we have truly dealt with these situations.

By going back to the intention that you set for yourself in reading this book, you will reconnect to what it is that you really want for yourself and your life. Through keeping this intention in mind, you have the ability to make the choice to go back into the past and uncover situations that may be serving as blockages for you from achieving the ideal life you would like to have. It may be beneficial to use your journal at this moment to set another more specific intention for why you are going back to the past; essentially to heal your wounds and receive the closure you never received in hopes of not having those instances serve as roadblocks anymore in your life.

Before you set your intention, I would like you to turn to the next page of your journal and answer the following questions. They may help you get more clarity on what it is that you would like to achieve.

(1) What do you feel you need to do in order to clean up your past?

(2) What things would have to happen in order for you to feel like you truly put the past behind you?

(3) Make a list of the things that you feel would have to happen in order for your past to be cleaned up.

(4) Do you think there are any particular conversations that need to happen with others in order for you to move on from your past?

(A) The Power Of Creating A Personal Timeline To Help Clean Up Your Past

Oftentimes the questions I just asked you above may be quite difficult to answer just off the top of your head, especially if you have been so used to putting things behind you for numerous years. This is where the idea of creating a Personal Timeline comes into play.

What I mean when I say create a Personal Timeline is that I want you to go back into your past and in a sense study yourself. Find old pictures, videos, old diary or journal entries, old school projects or/and anything that you have from your past. If for whatever reason you do not have anything like this from your past, that is okay. There are questions below that will allow you to connect with your past, regardless of if you have items from that time or not.

If you do have items though, I would suggest you lay them out in the chronological order of your life to really begin to see and reconnect with your younger self throughout numerous ages. It is through this that you can begin to learn more about who you were and how you have come to be who you are today. It will also possibly allow you to figure out when and where your preoccupation with your body, your weight, calories, food and exercise may have occurred.

This exercise is very powerful because through actually reconnecting with old videos, pictures or items that allow you to begin to emotionally connect to those younger versions of yourself you can begin to get an indication of which times and parts of your life you feel need healing.

I know for myself, whenever I look at certain pictures when I am nine, ten, eleven and twelve as well as eighteen, nineteen, twenty and twenty-one, I am instantly brought back to the extreme pain that I was experiencing during those years. From my reaction to those pictures, I knew that those were particular times in my life for me to go back to and do some healing exercises. I am going to list a few exercises you can do below.

By creating a timeline and "studying" yourself you are able to reconnect with those past emotions and again create awareness that their existence still resides inside of you, and in particular is still connecting with that inner child. It is through this exercise that you can first begin to pinpoint particular times and instances where you experienced pain and are in need of healing.

As I mentioned above, before you begin your timeline journey I would like you to set an intention for why are you doing this. Oftentimes when we are not clear of our intention behind why we are engaging in particular behaviors or actions we can become unmotivated to continue. If things get rough or uncomfortable along the way, having a clear intention as to why you are even engaging in those particular activities or making those particular choices is quite beneficial for you to turn to and remind yourself of your bigger goal. Before you actually dive into beginning your personal timeline, I would like you to set your intention.

You can answer this by asking yourself the following questions,

- Why am I even going back into the past at all?
- What am I hoping to accomplish by going back into the past?
- What am I hoping to achieve by creating a timeline and studying myself in a sense?

Your answer may be something like this:

> My intention for creating this timeline is to uncover the particular instances where my inner child or my younger self still feels unheard, sad, not validated, scared, confused, angry or unloved. I intend on recognizing those instances in my past where which that younger me does not feel closure in order to take the necessary steps to heal my past. This in turn will allow me to have the life I always imagined was possible.

Questions to Ask Around Your Personal TimeLine

Once you begin to uncover some things about yourself from your past and have begun to study yourself, it may be beneficial for you to answer the following questions. Through answering these questions you may begin to learn more about yourself and recognize what areas are in need of healing.

Answer the following questions based on the time of your life when you were 1-10 years old.

(1) What type of person were you during this age range?

(2) What was your personality like during this age range?

(3) What did you want to be when you grew up during this time/what was your job at this time?

(4) What activities did you like to do during these years? What were you passionate about? What were you interested in?

(5) What was your relationship with your family like during this age range?

(6) What was your relationship with your friends like during this age range?

(7) Did you have any romantic relationships during this age range? Crushes? What were these relationships like?

(8) What was your opinion of your appearance when you were in this age range?

(9) Did you like yourself at this time? Did you have a positive self-esteem? Why or why not?

(10) Did you like the way you looked? Why or why not?

(11) What parts of your body did you love? Why?

(12) What parts of your body did you wish could

have been different? Why? What do you wish they could look like? Why?

(13) Were you concerned about your weight during this age range? Why or why not?

(14) Depending on the time that you went through puberty, how did that time and change to your physical body affect you?

(15) Were you excited with your new appearance and body parts? Why or why not?

(16) If you looked at your body as being a separate part from yourself, at what age did this start?

(17) If you became somewhat disconnected from your body and started to view it as something you no longer related to, knew and/or liked, when did this disconnection from your body begin?

(18) How did you feel about yourself when you were being seen in a bathing suit during this age range?

(19) What was your relationship with food like at this time? Did you ever diet during this age range? Why or why not?

If you have dieted before, please answer the following questions:

(20) Why did you begin to diet? How old where you?

(21) What were you hoping to achieve from dieting?

(22) How long did your diets last?

(23) What type of diets were they?

(24) Did anyone know you were on a diet? Why or why not?

(25) Did you ever use laxatives? Diet Pills? Over exercise? Binge? Purge? Restrict? If so at what age did this happen and why?

(26) Did you ever avoid going to particular places because you were going to be seen in a bathing suit? If so what were these places? How do you think that wanting to avoid these places affected your life during this age range?

(27) Were there any activities you participated in where which your physical body was highly involved during this age range? If yes, please explain what activities they were. Did you need to have a particular body type to continue in these activities or were there ideas around what your physical body should look like? If yes, please explain. Did this ever cause you to think differently about your body?

(28) Were there any activities you participated in where which your physical appearance was highly involved during this age range? If yes, please explain what activities they were. Did you need to have a particular appearance to continue in these activities or were there ideas around what

your physical appearance should look like? If yes, please explain. Did this ever cause you to think differently about your appearance?

(29) Do you think you still view yourself, internally and/or externally, in the same way in which you did during this particular age range? Why or why not?

(30) Were there ever comments made about yourself, internally and/or externally, that hurt your feelings and stuck in your mind? If so, what were these comments? Do these comments still ruminate in your mind today? Are these comments a part of the story you have been telling yourself for years?

FINAL QUESTIONS:

As a result of answering all of these questions, have you gained any new awareness or insight to your younger self? If so please explain what this new awareness is. If not please explain so as well.

Based on the answers you've given, have you discovered any particular moments or instances that are in need of healing? If so please explain what these moments are. If not please explain as well.

Repeat those exact same questions for the following age ranges:

- Ages 10-15
- Ages 15-20
- Ages 20-30
- Ages 30 +

(B) The Power Of Writing To Help Clean Up Your Past

After you have created your timeline and established particular instances that feel incomplete and in need of healing to you, you have the opportunity to begin to heal those experiences. One way to achieve healing of your past is through writing.

i.   *Using Your Journal As A Means To Express Your Inner Child/Younger Self*

By using your journal you can begin to connect with that younger version of yourself and reflect on particular moments and instances where you feel incomplete. Allow that younger part of yourself to come up and express herself. Allow her to say exactly what she needs to say to you. If she is angry let that anger show. If she is sad allow her to be sad. If she is disappointed and scared allow that to come through her words. This is her opportunity to let anything and everything she is feeling inside to be expressed. Don't hold back – now is the time to let it all out.

ii.   *Writing Letters To Your Inner Child/*
      Younger Self

After you have allowed your younger self to express
herself to you in your journal writing, you can respond
to this younger self by writing her a letter. I would
suggest that you address the letter to your younger
self, i.e. Paula at age ten. If you have access to pictures
from your past, set the picture of yourself from whatever age you are writing the letter to beside you. Begin
to connect with yourself at that particular age; go back
to your journal and read what she expressed. Through
writing this letter, you now have the opportunity to
respond to her words and let her know that you hear
and understand her. You can express to her that you
recognize that she is experiencing pain and discomfort, but she need not worry anymore as you are going
to take over now by not only protecting her but by taking care of her from here on out. You can even use this
letter as a means to apologize to her any way you feel
is necessary. I would suggest that you express everything that you wish someone else had said to you at
that age that would have left you feeling heard, understood and consoled.

Here is a journal entry of mine that even though it is
not outlined in the same way that I have just asked

you to do the exercise, I was still connecting to my inner child. I wanted to share the power that connecting with your younger self has in the healing process.

November 20.2007
I owe it to the little girl inside of me
I owe it to the little girl inside of me to fix myself, figure out why I behaved the way I did in the past and forgive her. Tell her that she was just a child and didn't know any better. Let her know that she wasn't perfect but that no one is perfect, but that she was all right, she wasn't much different than anyone else, just had her own set of issues. She didn't know why she got so nervous and anxious all the time; she believed that was the way everyone felt.
But now she knows better.
Now she realizes she was different in that way and she can't blame herself for that lack of knowledge. Now that she knows the truth, she's trying to fight those nerves and anxiety and not keep repeating the self-destructing behavior with food. She knows that food won't take away that anxiety, though it may relieve it for a moment. She now knows that her relationship with him or her too won't take away that anxiety, though it may block it at that moment too. But she also knows the way she feels after she binges, guilt, disgust, embarrassment and hatred towards herself. Yet, she kept doing it over and over and over and over again.

Why?

We now know why. Lack of self-love.

She didn't think she deserved any better. She truly believed there was no way out. But now she knows better and all that matters is that she is trying. You have to give yourself credit for trying because you could be eating the food and you could be with the boy, but you are not, you are fighting little girl. You put your foot down and you won't turn back. You made a decision and promised yourself that you are going to be better, because you deserve better and I am not letting you disappoint yourself AGAIN.

There is no, I'll just start tomorrow. Or just one last time won't hurt.

How many times have you said that to yourself? Too many, and you know that you never listen. You know that tomorrow may never come.

You need to stop now; you need to love yourself NOW. You need to treat yourself like you would console a confused best friend. You are your best friend, don't you see little one?

(C) The Power Of Visualizations To Help Clean Up Your PastYour Past

Another powerful exercise you can do in regards to healing your inner child is through visualization.

Before you begin to do these visualization exercises, it is really important for you to choose a place where you feel completely comfortable, both physically and mentally. Once you have found a place you like, take a comfortable seat or even lye on your back, with your eyes closed. Just like we did with the writing exercises through journaling and writing letters, I would like you to go back to a time where your inner child is experiencing pain. Allow your inner child to speak, if she needs to cry, cry, if she needs to scream, scream, etc. Just allow her to let everything out. Have her describe the scenario as best as she can and allow yourself to go back into that time of your life as best as you are able to.

Now I want you to visualize that time of your life that your younger self is describing and see exactly what she looks like. Where is she? I want you to envision your current self is now sitting down beside her. Similarly to what I suggested in the letters, allow your current self to say exactly what you wish your inner child heard at that moment of her life.

Tell her that she no longer needs to be upset, mad, or scared as you are there, as you love her, and you are going to protect her from now onwards.

Tell her that she is beautiful, smart and good enough

for anything she desires.

Tell her that she is deserving of love from others as well as from herself.

Tell her that she is worthy, capable, strong, and absolutely perfect just as she is, inside and out.

Allow your inner child to really hear those words. Now I want you to envision your inner child and your current self, hugging. After you feel the hug has ended and your younger self/inner child feels consoled, tell her to go off and engage in some sort of activity that she finds pleasure in. The goal of this is to visualize the end of this scene with your inner child in a safe and enjoyable place such as playing in the backyard, going for a walk by the water or sleeping peacefully in her bed. Just make sure you end the scene in a way that is meaningful for you, since you know what makes you feel safe and happy.

I walked a number of my clients through this visualization exercise and each of them told me how much they got out of it. By allowing themselves to connect with their inner child and tell her exactly what they wished they had heard at the age that we were working on, a level of healing and connection automatically took place. As mentioned earlier, crying is a good thing and if you can allow yourself to cry the tears of your younger self, like all of my clients have done when I walked them through this exercise. You again are releasing old stored up emotions and feelings.

I always ensured that before I finished walking my clients through this visualization exercise, that we closed off that memory in a way that felt safe to them. Similar to the examples that I used above, I ensured that my clients left their younger selves in a safe and happy place.

You can repeat this same exercise for as many times, scenarios and ages that you feel would benefit from this type of acknowledgment and healing.

(D) The Power Of Healing Ceremonies To Help Clean Up Your Past

Another thing you can do to clean up the past is to perform a Healing Ceremony. Similar to what you did in regards to writing in your journal, writing letters and through the visualization exercises, start by choosing one period in your life where your inner child does not feel healed. If you have pictures from that time and/or any sort of memorabilia, you can set it all up in a place you feel you want to perform your Healing Ceremony. Just like with the writing exercises, it may be beneficial for you to set (and write) an intention as to why you are performing this Healing Ceremony to begin with.

For example, when I turned twenty-five years old, I felt a very big desire to put closure to the first quarter of my life. Therefore, rather than just focusing on one particular instance where my inner child felt incomplete, my intention was to put closure on my past and start fresh in a sense, from age twenty-five onwards.

I went around my house and found pictures and other memorabilia from the first twenty-five years of my life that I felt held particular significance. I lit candles and played a song that held meaning for me, as well as, represented exactly what I was looking to accomplish at that time. While the music was playing and the candles were lit, I took each picture and piece of memorabilia and placed it on my bed inside of the room I grew up in. I looked at the pictures and memorabilia while the song played and really reconnected to my past as much as I was able to. When the song was over, I again set the intention I had for myself and blew out the candles. It was a very powerful experience and something that I felt gave me real closure.

You can almost think of the Healing Ceremony as a cleanse in a sense. Cleansing away past emotions, negative memories or anything that may still be weighing you down. It's important to remind yourself that you want to heal your past, with the goal of finding peace around that particular time frame.

I would suggest that you too light candles, play music that you find inspires you or is related to your intention in your Healing Ceremony, burn sage and/or incense that you enjoy or that may have significance to the concept of letting things go and healing the past as well. When it comes to a location for your Healing Ceremony, you can choose any particular place that speaks to you and holds value to your overall intention.

Just remember there is no right or wrong way to perform a healing ceremony, all that matters is that you do it and receive the intention you desire.

(E) The Power Of Forgiveness To Help Clean Up Your Past

Up until now we have focused a lot on cleaning up of the past around situations involving primarily you. Within these exercises you may have noticed that you asked your younger self for forgiveness. It is through the process of forgiveness that we are able to allow our younger selves to experience not only the healing and closure of that particular experience, but also experience the feeling of connection and trust in ourselves once again.

What I mean by this is oftentimes if we have been living our lives in a particular manner where we have allowed others or ourselves to treat us in any other way than we truly deserve. We may have lost trust in our own ability to protect ourselves from any sort of harm, whether that be emotional, physical, mental or otherwise. This lack of trust results in a disconnection from our true selves and we may begin to unconsciously no longer value or see ourselves in a light that we may have viewed ourselves in years prior.

Think of it – when you were a kid how did you react when someone stole your toy from you? How did you react when someone said something mean to you? Most probably, you cried, screamed or got angry as an automatic result of knowing that you were not treated properly.

Now I am not saying that screaming, yelling or crying automatically when someone does something wrong to you is what we should strive for. What I am getting at by saying this is that when we were children, there was an innate reaction in us to protect ourselves and to feel some sort of feeling towards our own worthiness. The same can be said towards ourselves. When we engage in behavior that is not in alignment to what we know we are truly deserving and worthy of, we may begin to lose trust towards ourselves along the way. It is through these acts where there is a lack of trust, respect, love, direct from others or ourselves, that we may begin to disconnect from ourselves furthermore and allow ED to take over.

With this knowledge in mind, when we are in the manner of cleaning up our past, the concept of forgiveness holds a very valuable and essential part of the healing process. I am referring to forgiveness not only towards ourselves and from others, but forgiving others as well.

We can use this same type of mentality when it comes to the people or instances in our lives where we feel incomplete. Through creating yourself a personal timeline, you may have been brought back to particular incidences or times where you felt that you were treated improperly by others or where you actually treated others in a manner you do not feel good about. These instances are opportunities for you to take action when it comes to the aspect of forgiveness.

If you felt that someone did something to you and you have not been able to move on or let go, where that story about *"they did this to me"* or *"it is their fault"* or *"I still can't believe they did that to me"* is entrenched in your mind, I would confidently say that you have an opportunity to forgive them.

When I say that you may automatically react by saying something like, *"well they don't deserve my forgiveness or I have no desire to allow them to know that I have forgiven them."* Regardless of what comes up for you as a reaction to this statement that I just made, it is important to note that without forgiving others in your life, you are actually the one who ends up suffering – not them.

Without forgiveness you are the one who continues to suffer, as you stay captive to the instance and the pain through your own thoughts and the fact that you cannot let go. Learning how to forgive involves learning how to let go of the areas where ED has attached himself. Things that were *"done wrong to you"*. Things that ultimately keep you, and not necessarily the other person, stuck in suffering.

Learning how to forgive another in the end has to do with *you* as it allows you to establish a sense of freedom. For when you forgive, you release yourself from the constraints that keep you pulled down and locked inside of an uncomfortable prison held within your mind by ED.

Forgiveness results in allowing your mental, physical and emotional body to let go of that story where you were hurt. It essentially releases ED from continuing to keep you trapped as a victim to your experiences and makes room for you to move forward with your life by no longer being stuck in your past.

Again, ED may show up all prideful and say, *"I don't want to contact that person because they might say this or that person doesn't deserve to hear from me, they should be the one contacting me!"*

Bottom line, ED is full of excuses as to why things cannot workout the way you truly wish they could. By creating a separation from ED you begin to see the ability you truly have in making different decisions by *CHOOSING* not to listen to ED's words.

With those common thoughts that ED says, you again have the option to make a *CHOICE*. You can *CHOOSE* to let ED's prideful ways be in control and *CHOOSE* not to contact whoever you feel you need to talk to about what's bothering you. As a result, you will stay stuck where you are, controlled by ED and having a very difficult time fully moving forward with your life, as there is baggage from the past pulling you back. You could also *CHOOSE* to do whatever you felt it took to clear up that issue with that individual through taking the necessary steps that are completely separated from ED's opinion.

Depending on your particular situation sometimes engaging in a conversation with someone you have unresolved issues with is not the best choice. It is important to note that forgiveness does not even have to occur in the manner where the other person is even involved. Forgiveness can take place within the realm of your own self.

Before choosing what steps to take, really ask your-self would this *CHOICE* be for my best benefit, pride aside, or would interacting with that person only cause more pain and damage?

I know for myself, my first boyfriend and I had a lot of unresolved issues after we broke up. As I began this process of gaining awareness of ED, it was very clear that during our relationship I wasn't entirely myself based on the fact that I was living my life with an ED who was also an Eating Disorder. As the years passed, I knew I still had a lot of pain and anger toward our situation and with him that I felt was holding me back from fully moving forward with my life.

Even though I was scared to contact him about this, I knew that *CHOOSING* to connect with him and ask for his forgiveness for what I had done wrong to him was an essential part in cleaning up this part of my past. Asking for forgiveness was a lot easier for me then forgiving him for all *"the wrong he had done to me,"* again because ED continued to tell me the story that I cannot forgive him for doing those things to me, and so on.

When I pushed those thoughts aside and began to understand that by holding onto the story of the past, the experiences where I felt he treated me poorly and unfairly, I was the one who was suffering, not him.

When I *CHOOSE* to step outside of the situation and no longer allowed ED to be so attached to it, and realize that my ex, like myself, is a human being trying to figure himself and life out as well, someone who makes mistakes just like I do along the way, my anger and pain lessened. My attachment to this situation began to change as I no longer felt the way ED had convinced me to feel all of those years – like a helpless victim.

I was ready to finally release myself from the ED's played out story of how I was treated wrong. I knew that in order to truly move forward in the way I wanted, where I was in love with myself, my body and my life, *CHOOSING* to forgive him was highly important.

What forgiving him also allowed me to do was forgive myself for allowing someone to treat me that way. I forgave myself for not realizing at the time that I deserved to be treated with respect and love. I forgave myself for participating in a dysfunctional relationship, but I knew that this relationship was a reflection of the internal relationship that I had with myself, my body and food.

With that forgiveness came a sense of freedom I had not consciously ever experienced. I believe that forgiveness is one of the keys to reconnecting with our true selves, because in order to get to that place, ED is now nowhere to be found.

Again, it may be beneficial for you to set an intention as to why you are *CHOOSING* to forgive those in your life who still evoke incomplete feelings. In the example I just shared with you, my intention was to clean up my past and not let an old relationship and unresolved issues keep me stuck there. My intention was to free myself from that experience, which in my mind meant that I would be open and ready to let the kind of love and relationship that I knew I deserved to receive from another man come into my life, when it was the right time.

For my particular situation speaking to my ex was the best CHOICE for me to achieve my intention. As I mentioned before, depending on what your situation is that is not always necessary. Once you set that intention you can ask yourself whether or not you feel that speaking to those individuals in person is something that will better serve your intention or if simply engaging in some of the exercises listed below on your own will allow this intention to be met.

As mentioned earlier, this notion of forgiveness is also related to the parts of your life where you feel that you need to ask others for their forgiveness, as I felt with my ex-boyfriend. Again, ED may show up and try to stop you from asking for others' forgiveness because you are potentially going to be in a state of vulnerability, where which people may not forgive you or even be upset with you.

When asking for forgiveness from others, the important thing to remember is your bigger intention in doing this. By remembering that you are unable to control how other people will act or behave, you can walk into this interaction without any expectations. The goal here is to express to the other person how you are feeling and if necessary, apologize for every-

thing that you feel you might have done wrong.
Once again, the thing to remember here is your intention in asking for forgiveness from others to begin with – essentially to clean up your past and to leave you feeling that you have done everything that you could have from your end to close this instance or relationship on a positive note. Similar to what I stated in the concept of forgiving others, depending on the situation you may not be able to actually contact that person and ask for their forgiveness. This should not detract you from trying to gain healing of this instance. You can use some or all of the exercises below to gain forgiveness involving others as well.

Depending on your particular situation there are different options to *CHOOSE* from which will allow you to engage in forgiveness.

i. *The Power of Writing A Letter For Forgiveness*

Regardless if you want to forgive someone else or ask for forgiveness from another, I believe that writing a letter is a very important part of this process as it allows you to truly get connected to whatever it is that is still bothering you about this situation. You can *CHOOSE* to write a letter to that person and say everything you feel you still need to say to them in hopes of releasing it from you and feeling complete closure of this experience.

Depending on how you feel you can *CHOOSE* from the following:

(A) Give the letter to them in person and read it to them or allow them to read it while you are there

(B) Call them on the phone and read them the letter so you feel you have said everything you feel and are completely clear

(C) Mail them the letter and allow them to read it on their own

(D) Do not give them the letter but do some sort of Healing Ceremony around destroying the letter, where you set an intention for letting this go, letting this be released from you and emerging free

I would say that none of these ways are better or worse than the others. All that is important to note is that you want to ensure that you are not allowing fear – ED – to dictate your *CHOICE*. Now is the time to do whatever you need to do in hopes of truly feeling released from the power that this experience is still holding onto you.

Once that forgiveness has taken place, ED has a lot

less to say, as most of the stories he has been saying up until now are just repetitions from the days, weeks, months or years before.

When this forgiveness has taken place, a space opens up and allows you to be able to breathe a little bit deeper, see things a bit clearer and allows you to be able to be more aligned with yourself, the self that is separate from ED.

Once the past is cleaned up you have nothing stopping you. You are free to create your future from your authentic self, not from a place of fear and EGO, but rather from yourself. Your authentic self. In the exercise I just suggested above, forgiveness is often a key factor in truly receiving closure over our experiences. Forgiveness of and from others and forgiveness of ourselves. By taking these steps we can truly begin to close the past in a different way than it may have been closed before.

I suggest that if you feel like you have ever mistreated your body through name calling, criticizing, beating it up emotionally or hurting it physically through food, purging, or other forms of self-harm, that you perform these exercises around obtaining forgiveness from it. This is a very powerful part of truly changing your relationship with body and beginning to fall in love with it. One of my journal entries from a few years ago describes what I've realized about this process.

*

February 17.2008
A bit of forgiveness
Apologize to your body for all the shit you have put it through, all the self-destruction, all the verbal and physical beating it has endured. You ask yourself why it never listened to anything you said, why it seemed to always look the opposite of which you wish it did.

Think about it. When you punish a child does it get up and become the best kid the next day? When you treat something, someone with love, from a place of acceptance, change is surely available. Change is actually something you can embark on together. Rather than being in this constant fight with your body where you hate it for not losing the twenty pounds that you want to lose in the matter of a week, you need to be patient; you need to realize that if you take care of the inner you first, the outer you will surely follow.

Once you are able to love your body as it is now, your body will shape into the form that you desire. If you are coming from a place of true love and total acceptance, you and your body can go on the path together to become who you want to be. No hatred is accepted, no self-abuse is allowed. It will never get you to the place you hope to be. This is not just in relation to your body, but to your relationships in your life, with family members, co-workers, with your friends, your lovers and your overall self-acceptance.

You also have to have realistic goals. You need to know what your body is and what it isn't. You need to love and accept that. I know this may seem hard to do; it was and oftentimes still is for me. I always wished I could have super skinny thighs, but I never have, NEVER my entire life. I always carried my meat on my thighs and hips. I would stare in the mirror and see them and say ewwwww-wwwwwwwllllllll to myself over and over.

But now I laugh at ED's voice. I say, yeah you are right I don't have super skinny thighs, but I have a great heart, and a caring personality, nice eyes and a bright smile. ED makes you focus on the negatives always. He convinces you that you cannot say good things about yourself. Well I tell ED to shove it where the sun don't shine and to look at you and try to see what others see about you.

For years people would compliment my eyes and ED would say, They say that to everyone, it doesn't really mean anything. I would believe him. Until one day I REALLY looked at my eyes, no make-up just MY EYES and *thought, Whoa they are pretty!*

You know what happened that was even better than realizing I had pretty eyes? It's that it didn't matter. No one thought I was conceited. No one said that I was wrong. That's what ED tries to convince you into believing. He tries to make you think that you are wrong for saying anything nice about yourself, but the opposite is the truth. There is something wrong in not saying something nice about you.

*

I do recognize that this whole concept of forgiveness may be a very powerful and overwhelming experience, and oftentimes trying to do this alone is quite difficult.

As I have mentioned a few times in this book, feel free to reach out to me at www.paulagalli.com to help support you during this process. This leads directly to my next point, which I feel is quite necessary in helping you clean up your past.

(F) The Power Of Seeking Out Individuals Who Can Help You Clean Up Your Past

From answering all of the questions and doing all of the exercises that I have presented to you in the book so far, you may be feeling a bit overwhelmed in working through this entire process on your own. Alternatively, you may not be feeling overwhelmed at all but would still like to have a professional who is trained in the area of healing to help guide and assist you through this precious and important part of your life.

Depending on what you feel will be beneficial for you, you may want to see a Psychologist, a Therapist, a Naturopath, a Reiki Master, an Energy Healer, a Life Coach, a Minister or any other individual that you find will be able to help you deal with whatever you need guidance and support with. Oftentimes there are negative stereotypes around the idea of getting help from others. These stereotypes are usually around the idea of someone being labeled as weak, unstable or even crazy. I couldn't disagree more with these stereotypes, as I believe the individuals who reach out for help and guidance are not only truly powerful, but are also very self-aware. I see people who reach out for help and guidance as being very strong, because oftentimes asking for help and admitting we don't have it all figured out or together is quite challenging, especially in our society. Certain cultures also have particular ideas and stereotypes around what receiving help means.

All of these ideas are once again just the working of ED – who is at play not only in you and me as individuals but also in society at large.

Regardless of how you feel about reaching out for help, I believe that at the end of the day this is your life, no one else's. So once again, you have the *CHOICE* to do whatever it is that you want.

Remember at the beginning of this section I said that there were two *real* reasons why behavioral changes were not taking place and sticking in your life? The exercises listed above addressed the first reason, which was related to the fact that your past was not healed.

The second reason I listed, which I will address in the next section, was in regards to that fact that your thoughts are not in alignment to what you are currently trying to bring and attract into your life. In this next section I will focus on just that – learning how to change, alter and select your thoughts.

Recap:
In order to truly fall in love with yourself, your body and your life it is imperative that you clean up your past. Creating a personal timeline, writing, visualizations, performing Healing Ceremonies and forgiveness exercises are things you can do in order to heal your past. Oftentimes cleaning up the past is very difficult to do on our own. You may find it beneficial to

seek out individuals who can help you heal your past.

(1) I AM AWESOME EXERCISE!

Before we move onto the next section I really want you to take this moment to recognize all of the great work you just did again! Now tell yourself, "I am awesome!" Say it twice more and really believe it!

(2) I LOVE MYSELF EXERCISE!

Similarly to the same intention that I had you doing with the, "I am awesome" exercise, I would like you to say out loud to yourself, "I love myself." Say it twice more and really believe it!

Now I would like you to list 2 reasons why you love yourself.

"I love myself because _____
_____
_____."

"I love myself because _____
_____
_____."

(5) CHOOSE a Different Language To Speak – Separate From ED's

Up until this point, you have learned that inside each and everyone of us, there is an ED who automatically speaks a certain way based on our past. In this process of learning about ED you have not only begun to gain the awareness of his existence but have also begun to take the necessary steps to create a life separate from him.

ED's existence can also be recognized and known as our conditioned thoughts. It is important to notice that the thoughts that we are saying to ourselves daily hold enormous power in directing every single one of our choices, behaviors and actions. It is our thoughts that hold an enormous ability to truly change and direct our lives in the manner we would like them to go. When our thoughts are not in alignment to what we are currently trying to bring and attract into our lives, even with all of this newfound awareness of ED's existence, we will still continue to live a life that may feel quite similar to what it was before – unsatisfying and unfulfilled.

You may have noticed by now that ED has his own language that is founded in fear. When you hear the common phrases listed below, you should have the indication that this is ED speaking.

"I *should* _____."
"I *have* to do __x__ or be like ___y__"
"I *need* to _____."
"I am *too afraid* to _____."

Those are just some examples from ED's vocabulary. They are quite easy to detect since they are all founded in fear. As I mentioned in the first section of the book, I believe that an Eating Disorder is simply just a part of one's EGO that speaks a particular language, the Eating Disorder Language. Depending on where you lie on this spectrum, this language ED speaks changes accordingly. If your ED is also an Eating Disorder, then some or all of the phrases below may seem common to you. Even if your ED is not an Eating Disorder you may still relate to some of these examples.

"That food is good. That food is bad."
"I am not allowed to eat that."
"I can only eat that food because it will keep me thin."
"I cannot eat carbs because they will make me fat."
"I cannot eat fat."
"I am not allowed to wear those clothes."

"If I eat this way then people with think ___x___ of me."

"If I just eat perfectly and lose the weight then I will be happy."

"I am not good enough."

"I am fat."

"I hate my body." (i.e. "I hate my thighs." "I hate my stomach.")

"I wish I looked like ___x___"

"I need to lose weight."

"I need to go on another diet again."

"I already messed up by eating a cookie, I might as well just binge and eat it all tonight; I will just start fresh tomorrow."

"I messed up anyways today, so I might as well just keep eating like this and start fresh tomorrow or on Monday, or the at the beginning of the month."

"I need to be the best at everything I do."

"Unless I am the best, I suck."

"I have to be perfect."

"My body is too fat."

"If I eat I am weak."

"If I eat what I actually want I am weak."

"I am greedy if I eat what I want or too much."

"_x_ doesn't like me/this isn't working because I am too fat."

"I need to burn ___x___ many calories today or

else I am not good enough."

"I need to eat only this many calories today or else I am fat."

"I need to work out every day for at least ___x___ amount of time to make sure I don't get fat."

"I need to burn off all the calories I ate today/in that meal/in that dessert."

"When I lose weight I will finally be happy."

"I'm not fit enough to go to the gym."

"I'm not sick enough to have an Eating Disorder."

"Skinnier people are viewed as better."

"I'll do ___x___ when I lose ___y___ amount of pounds." *(i.e. "I'll buy new pants when I lose twenty pounds." "I'll go swimming when I lose 10 pounds." "I'll go to the gym when I lose 5 pounds.")*

Whether any of these particular examples resonate with you or not, ED has a way of creating rules in our lives through our thought processes. If you find yourself using the words: *can't, should/shouldn't, have to, need to, ought to,* or anything else that you find has taken your own personal *CHOICE* out of the picture, or anything that involves putting yourself down and does not stem from a place of positive self-TALK (self-trust, self-acceptance, self-love, self-knowledge), then

I can guarantee that it is ED who is speaking and in control, not the real you.

Remember – you were not born into this world with a tag on your foot indicating that you were going to treat yourself poorly or be filled with rules of who you should be or shouldn't be. You were born as a pure innocent child, filled with an abundance of love, who had the potential to be anyone you wanted to be.

You can think of it this way: Would you ever speak to your best friend or your child in this manner? I am guessing your answer is no! Well then why is it okay for you to speak towards yourself in this light? Why do you have to listen to and process everything that you would never say to someone else? Well I am here to say that you don't have to and you deserve not to.

In this section I want to focus on changing your internal dialogue through teaching you how to *CHOOSE* to speak a different language than ED's language. I want to invite you to *CHOOSE* to speak a language filled with compassion, understanding, patience, forgiveness and that is stemming from a place of positive self-TALK (self-trust, self-acceptance, self-love, self-knowledge). Just like it would take a lot of practice and time to learn how to speak a new language, such as Italian or Chinese, it is going to take the same amount of time and dedication to learn this new language – essentially the positive self-TALK language. It is through learning how to speak to yourself in this manner that your life will begin to truly shift in ways you always dreamed was possible. For it is through creating these different ways of thinking about and towards yourself, your body and your life, that you not only will begin to create a separation from ED by challenging his beliefs, but you will actually also begin to create new thought pathways in your brain. The first way that I feel you can begin to create your new language, separate from ED's, is through using positive affirmations.

(A) Setting Positive Affirmations

I would like you to list five things that you do not like about yourself, addressing both internal and external qualities.

1.
2.
3.
4.
5.

You may have just wondered why I asked you to list

five things you do not like about yourself. Well the reason I did that is because those are five thoughts we can focus on changing and ultimately eliminating from your life through the use of Positive Affirmations.

Positive Affirmations are specific thoughts that you purposely tell yourself to say. What you may have noticed from doing all of the exercises in this book is that you have a lot of thoughts. It is important to note that you can only think one thought at a time. By being aware of your current thoughts, like the five you just listed above, you now have the ability to *CHOOSE* whether or not you want to continue thinking those particular thoughts or not.

For example, if one of your thoughts above was, *"I hate my thighs"*, then your affirmation would be something like, *"I love my thighs."*

I know it may seem really hard to say, *"I love my thighs"* if you do not feel that way at all. What I suggest that you do if you cannot bring yourself to say that is to say, *"I accept my thighs."* Acceptance is the first step towards truly falling in love with anything, whether that involves yourself, your body or your life. When we can truly accept what we are presented with, what our body currently looks like and who we are, we step outside of the mindset of ED who is constantly telling us that things need to be different.

You can even go back into the story that you wrote about yourself and see some of the things that ED has said about you. i.e. If one of the thoughts in your story was that, *"I am not good enough"*, then your affirmation would be something like, *"I love and accept myself just as I am."*

When creating Positive Affirmations, you just want to make sure that they are affirmative and written in the present tense.

When you begin to use Positive Affirmations in your life, it might be beneficial to think of them in the following way. If you decided that you wanted to get bigger biceps, would you think that simply lifting a twenty-pound weight fifty times would result in your bicep changing into what you wanted it to look like? Of course not! You would have to continue to lift that weight on a number of occasions in order for your muscle to change shape.

The same can be said about your thoughts. It is important to know that ninety-percent of what you thought yesterday you are going to think again today. That is why Positive Affirmations are so important –

they allow you to keep ED from automatically dictating his thoughts to you daily.

Yet, just because you are starting to say new thoughts once or twice a day, it doesn't mean that your mind is now automatically going to say those new thoughts daily. Just like you would need to practice speaking Italian everyday to truly learn how to speak the language, it also takes time and constant practice to build new automatic thoughts that eventually take over the old ones. Similarly to how you have to lift the 20lb. weight multiple times in order to get the bicep you desire, you need to say these new Positive Affirmations a number of times in order to create the mindset you desire.

You can think of Positive Affirmations as the weights in your "mindset gym", for it is in your "mindset gym" where you can truly begin to fall in love with yourself, your body, and your life. Something I often tell my clients is to change all of their passwords, such as their email, to Positive Affirmations. This is a quick and easy way to ensure that you are automatically stating your new affirmations daily!

I started using Positive Affirmations or Mantras, which I like to think are the same thing, back in 2005. My next journal entry showcases the power that they have in creating the life that you truly want. One that ED tries to convince you isn't possible.

*

January 19.2008
Gaining Self-Trust
How is it possible to regain trust towards somebody who has beaten and battered you for years and all of a sudden asks for you to just trust them again one day?

I really don't know if that's possible so I began testing myself which indirectly verified that I had to take the leap and trust this foreign voice as it promised self-love, self-respect and self-confidence. I really had nothing else to lose as I was already living in my very own version of hell and anything different than that place seemed appealing to me.

So I did it. I started telling myself I trusted myself over and over and over again, even though a part of me was screaming that no trust would ever develop. But if my past has taught me anything it is that I can indeed start to change my views about and towards myself as I first repeated love yourself for years when I hated everything about me and eventually self-love grew. Next came know yourself over and over where knowledge about my identity was nonexistent but I had the love that I created out of my depression to guide me to gain such self-knowledge, I hoped. Once I started repeating that Mantra, this knowledge about myself began pouring into my soul and out through my tears. ED was finally revealed to me. All the lies and promises were finally challenged and confronted – so I asked myself why if these two statements produced responses, should or would this next Mantra produce anything different?

I did not love myself but I grew to love
I did not know but soon after I acquired deep seated knowledge
I do not trust but eventually I shall

I believe that we all have it in us to prosper to who we long to be but without these three important things, we will not be able to attain our every dream and goal. I have always heard that you must believe in yourself to achieve your dreams but I never used to think that was possible, because in my mind others controlled my destiny through their depictions of me. This no longer holds true in my life as I am now gaining control and along with it trust. You too can do this as it is in every one of us to develop such self-belief. This will not make you conceited, which I always was scared of, but rather it makes you a content person with yourself and the world around you.

*

(B) Using The Mirror As A Means To Change Your Thoughts

The mirror is a very powerful place and holds a lot of emotion for many of us, for it is through the mirror that we connect with the reflection of ourselves, a reflection that oftentimes can become distorted by ED's influence.

For those of you that are also living with an ED who is an Eating Disorder, the mirror has probably been a place you would like to avoid altogether and the fact that I am even just talking about this may bring up negative feelings all by itself.

Though I do not want to disregard the feelings that you are experiencing when you are in front of the mirror, I do, however, want to let you know that it is plausible to change those feelings regarding your reflection.

What I have been teaching you so far in this section is the power of our thoughts. I believe that our feelings can change around our reflection in the mirror through using similar exercises to those I have just discussed around shifting your thoughts.

Taking these exercises to the mirror most certainly

does heighten the intensity of the experience and for many people they find it quite difficult to do. I encourage you to try your best at doing this, regardless of how uncomfortable or awkward you may feel. I can assure you that the more you practice this particular exercise the more comfortable it will become. It is important to remember that when you are in the process of creating a life separate from ED and truly beginning to fall in love with yourself, your body and your life, you are taking huge leaps outside of your comfort zone. It would only make sense that you would find some, if not all, of these exercises uncomfortable at first because you have never done them before. Similar to some of the earlier exercises, I suggest that you either go back and reconnect with your original intention as to what you would like to achieve from this overall process or that you create an entirely new intention around these mirror exercises.

Essentially what I would like you to do is create a daily routine that involves looking at yourself directly in the mirror for at least five minutes a day.

For some of you this may be very easy, for some it may be a bit challenging and for others this may be the hardest thing I have asked you to do up until this point. Regardless, I want you to take five minutes every day to look at yourself in the mirror and say the affirmations I have listed below. You will see a list of examples of affirmations you can say to yourself.

Alternatively, you can choose some of the new Positive Affirmations that you just wrote about above. The *CHOICE* is totally up to you.

- Remember, there is no right or wrong in doing this exercise.
- I suggest that you focus on one to three affirmations at a time in order to really allow your mind to process these new thought patterns that you want to instill long term within your mind.
- I also suggest that whichever Positive Affirmation you decided to use in your new email password, you also use in this exercise to keep things congruent.

Here Are Some Examples Of Positive Affirmations That You Can Use:

I love myself.
I love my body.
I accept myself.
I am good enough.
I am worthy.
I know myself.
I accept myself just as I am.

I accept my body just as it is.
I trust myself.
I respect myself.
I am perfect just as I am.
I am safe.
I trust.
I am calm.
I am taken care of.
I trust in the process of life.

Once you have chosen your one to three affirmations, I would like you to look at yourself in the mirror daily for at least five minutes and state them out loud.

I suggest that you also buy markers that can be written with and washed off of mirrors. Write these new affirmations on your mirror so whenever you are in the presence of your mirror, even if you are not saying the affirmations out loud like you are within that five minute daily period, you at least read them inside of your mind.

I suggest that you focus on the same one to three affirmations for at least one month and see what happens by the end of that month. If you find that those three affirmations are not only easy to say to yourself, but have now become automatic thoughts, then great, move onto the next affirmations that you want to bring into your life. If this is not the case, then continue working on those affirmations daily until you really begin to believe them. With practice and dedication it will happen, I promise.

I do want to acknowledge that I know for some of you this exercise seems absolutely impossible. You may feel it is a stretch for you to not only not say these thoughts out loud if you are standing in front of the mirror, but to even get yourself to really truly look at your own reflection in the mirror. If this is the case, I suggest you try again and then try one more time.

If you are truly unable to do this, then please ask someone who you trust and feel comfortable with to help you in this process, or if that isn't an option for you feel free to reach out to me at www.paulagalli.com and I would be more than happy to help you through this process to the best of my ability, for it is through being able to truly connect with yourself in the mirror that you will begin to know and feel that ED is no longer the one in the driver's seat.

(C) The Power Of Gratitude

As you have learned by now ED tends to focus on everything that isn't working in our lives. By continuing to follow down his negative path, we not only remain unhappy but we actually miss out on all of the wonderful things that we have in our lives that we could be grateful for.

For example, normally when ED speaks about our bodies he is focused on how things *should* look a certain way, how that part of your body *should* be smaller, tighter, more toned, or eliminated altogether. If we separate from ED we can begin to look at our bodies through a different lens which allows us to learn how to become truly grateful for our bodies ability to be able to move, to function and to assist us in living the best life possible. (i.e. To be grateful for our legs for allowing us to walk. To be grateful for our hands that allow us to eat, type on the computer, carry things, wave hello).

Not only do we have our beautiful and amazing body to be grateful for, but we have our health, the food that we eat, the relationships in our lives that support us, our home, our beds and our blankets that keep us warm at night. When you start focusing on all of the amazing things you already have in your life, not only do you begin to lift some new weight in your mindset gym but you truly begin to automatically fall in love with yourself, your body, and your life because you begin to see how blessed you actually are.

I suggest that you start each day and end each night by listing at least three things you are grateful for. Then watch how your life begins to change.

(D) In What Way(s) Are You Proud Of Yourself?

Another thing you can do before you go to bed is list off either out loud, within your mind or in your journal, five things that you are proud of yourself for doing that day. Oftentimes it is so much easier to focus on what we *didn't* do, what we *should* have done or what we *wished* we would have done, rather than focusing on all of the great things we did do. By training your mind to not only recognize, but **list at least five things that you are proud of yourself for doing each day,** you are automatically directing your thoughts to focus on the positive things about yourself. The more you do this, the more automatic it will be for you to think this way.

Some examples are:
> "I am proud of myself today because I went to sleep when I was tired."
> "I am proud of myself today because I ate what I wanted even when ED told me not to."
> "I am proud of myself today because I finished that paper I was working on."

"I am proud of myself today because I didn't over-eat like ED normally convinces me to do."
"I am proud of myself today because I listened to my body and went for a walk."
"I am proud of myself today because I wrote in my journal."

I know for some of you this exercise may be quite difficult. When we are living with ED he often convinces us that we are not allowed to focus on the things we do well, but rather focus on everything we could have done better. Remember that ED has unrealistic expectations of who he expects us to be. This reasoning comes from a fear of being just who we are, as ED always tells us we aren't good enough. He thinks you can be this "perfect" person. Everything you do is often compared to this idea that he has created around who this person *should* be, what this person *should* say and how this person *should* act. I always say to clients of mine, "Name me one person who is absolutely perfect." No one has ever been able to name somebody.

As a result of living your life this way, you miss out on realizing that you are not only good enough but that you are perfect just as you are now. By beginning to allow yourself to start recognizing and stating the things that you did throughout the day that you are proud of yourself for, you will not only begin to create a further separation from ED but will begin to truly fall in love with yourself, your body and your life.

Recap:

You can only truly think one thought at a time. Your thoughts stem from ED's opinion and language that he has been speaking to you for years. You have the *CHOICE* to speak whatever language you want by CHOOSING your thoughts. Positive affirmations, mirror exercises, gratitude exercises, and acknowledging what you are proud of yourself for each day can be a great way for you to begin to practice the ability that you have in *CHOOSING* your own language. It is through *CHOOSING* to think thoughts that are in alignment with loving yourself and your body that your life will begin to shift like you always wanted it to.

(6) Who Do You Admire and Why?

In the space below please answer the following questions.

Who do you admire and look up to in your life? They can be people you know such as family members, friends, teachers or acquaintances. They can also be people you do not know such as authors, researchers, speakers, athletes or celebrities. It is important to know that when answering this question, you do not need to admire everything about that person; maybe you just like some of their qualities.

Please describe each person you look up to and list all of the qualities and things you admire about them. The more specific you can be the better.

_____
_____
_____
_____
_____
_____
_____
_____
_____
_____
_____
_____
_____
_____

(7) Re-Discovering & Creating Your Ideal Self

I just asked you to describe all of the qualities that you admire about other people. You may have heard this before but the qualities you admire in others are actually qualities you have within yourself.

Now when you hear that, right away you may not agree and automatically say something like, *"Well that's not true. I am not like that person. I do not possess those qualities."* Even though you may feel like you do not possess those qualities that you admire in other's right now, doesn't mean that those qualities are not part of who you actually are. For it is usually the people that we look up to that possess the qualities that are most in alignment with our true selves. With this knowledge in mind, the following exercises will allow you to further separate yourself from ED, while you re-discover who you truly are and create who you would like to be. I believe a gentle combination of the two is highly beneficial in truly falling in love with yourself, your body and your life.

(A) Re-Discover Who You Already Were

Based on the personal timeline that you created earlier, you have gone back into your life and studied yourself, so to speak. When we are working on creating a life separate from ED, it is important to go back into our pasts and reconnect with ourselves, all the while discovering what we used to enjoy doing. Oftentimes, when we are living with ED as the main director of our lives we may have geared away from actually engaging in activities or hobbies that we used to enjoy.

With this knowledge in mind, I would like to ask you to turn to the next page of your journal and answer the following questions. You may already have some of these questions answered from previous exercises I have asked you. Feel free to use those responses here if you like.

I. How would you describe yourself as a child? What type of child were you? What qualities did you possess?

II. Do you believe that your current qualities are the same from when you were a kid? If not when did they change? What is different about your current qualities?

III. What activities did you like to do? What where some of your interests? What did you gain pleasure from doing? i.e. writing, reading, dancing, doing sports, painting, music, art, bike riding

IV. When you grew into an adolescent or preteen what did you enjoy doing then?

V. Do you still engage in those activities? If not, when did you stop doing these activities? Do you ever think about doing these activities again? What stops you from doing them now?

From answering those questions you may have realized that you used to engage in activities that you no longer do anymore. When looking back, you may have realized that some of those activities are still things you wish you were doing or would like to be doing, yet, you may no longer take the time to make them a part of your life. As we get older, ED often convinces us that a lot of things that we used to do as children or teenagers are not allowed as adults.

For example, maybe you used to love bike riding or swimming as a kid, but as you grew older ED convinced you that you were too busy to take the time to do those activities. Maybe other priorities took precedence in your life, such as work or school, and these activities slowly drifted out of your life. That is often what happens. None of this is bad or good, right or wrong. But it is important to note that this is still the workings of ED.

If this is the case for you I would highly suggest that you start to incorporate some, if not all, of those activities that you used to love doing into your daily life from here on out. Then I invite you to watch how you participating in these activities allows you to begin to automatically become more fulfilled, happier and feel connected with yourself in a way you have probably not felt for years. I believe that one of the ways that you reconnect with your true self is through a connection to childhood.

Children automatically choose things they enjoy doing and choose not to do things that they do not enjoy. For human beings, it is quite simple at the beginning. Yet, everything that we have been taught, alongside any personal hardships that we face throughout our childhood and adolescent years, shape us into who we believe we are today. As you have already learned from the beginning of this book, who you *think* you are today isn't necessarily who you *actually* are. As a result, this inner guidance that you had as a child, that automatically allowed you to connect to what you truthfully enjoyed doing has been pushed down and replaced by what you *should* be doing, essentially ED. By engaging in these activities that you used to love, such as bike riding or swimming, you may begin to reignite a part of yourself that you haven't been connected with in a long time. Through finding things that you absolutely love doing, that bring you joy and pleasure, it can spark the fire of our true selves to show up and allow us to create even further separation from ED.

I am very aware that engaging in these activities may result in ED to show up and almost judge what you are doing. He may say things like, *"Why are you doing this? You don't do this anymore. You haven't done this in years. This isn't a part of who you are. Why do you think you are allowed to do this activity? Who are you trying to be? These activities were only good for you when you were a child. You have more important things to do now. You are just wasting time. You should be doing something more important and productive."* If your ED says anything like this please realize that this is completely normal and expected.

This is also another opportunity for you to gain awareness of ED because as you begin to engage in these activities ask yourself the following questions,

- What thoughts are coming up for me?
- What is ED telling me about myself as I start to engage in this activity? (i.e. That I can't do it? That I am not allowed? That I am not good enough, skinny enough, worthy enough?)

ED lives in fear and since he has been the one who has been controlling you for all of these years, he is becoming fearful of the fact that you are *CHOOSING* to engage in activities that he did not recommend. It is through this *CHOICE*, alongside taking action and not allowing whatever ED says stop you from participating in that activity, that ED will begin to take a back seat in your life and the real you will begin to be the driver again; just like it was when you were a child.

Now that you have been able to re-discover who you were as a child and what you enjoyed doing, it is also important to think about the person you would like to be if ED no longer existed.

(B) Create Who You Want To Be

For many of you, the thought of creating a life separate from ED is very scary. You have lived with ED for as long as you have now and the thought of no longer speaking his particular language and following his rules and guidelines can leave you feeling fearful and lost. You may feel this way because you are unsure of who you are separate from ED. Even though living with ED may not have been the most pleasant experience, there has still been some comfort in having him around. In this sense you have become accustomed to feeling comfortably uncomfortable with ED in your life.

Again, this way of feeling is not only completely normal, but somewhat expected. Since ED has been such a powerful influence in your life; essentially you have connected yourself to being what ED dictates. Yet, you have learned that you do have the *CHOICE* of whether or not you want to continue allowing ED to be your identity or not.

If you are ready to begin to *CHOOSE* to live a life separate from ED, this next exercise will help. In this exercise I am going to ask you to think about the person you would want to be if ED was no longer in the picture. What type of life would you want to be living if ED wasn't around? Learning how to start thinking this way will further create separation from ED.

If you could be anybody who would that person be?

Let me be clear that when I am asking this question, I am not referring to if you could be anybody else, I am talking about if you could be any version of yourself, who would that person be? Who would your ideal self be? What would your ideal self be doing?

You may be thinking, *"I'm too afraid to write what I want down on paper, because what will happen if it doesn't work out or come true?"*

Being too afraid to write down what you really want for yourself and your life is quite common. ED may even come up with numerous excuses as to why you *can't do it* and use time, your presumed ability level or finances as reasons why what you really want is impossible. Your only job right now is to tell ED to take a back seat and get in tune with what you really desire for yourself.

After visualizing what it is you really want, choose to write it down regardless of what ED may be saying. Remember, ED shows up out of fear. Things such as fear of failure, fear of looking bad and fear of being judged by others are reasons why ED may try to stop you from writing down what you truly want. By choosing to write this down from a place of positive self-TALK, (self-trust, self-acceptance, self-love, self-knowledge) you are putting out your true desires to yourself and the universe around you, from a place of believing that your dreams are possible.

It is important to note that you don't have to know *how* what you want will work out you. The goal of this exercise is not about the *how*. It is about practicing to ask for what you *truly want* to bring into your life without ED's influence guiding you and furthermore, beginning to *believe* that it is even a possibility.

Answering any or all of the following questions may help you with this exercise.

What is your ideal relationship with yourself, your body, your weight, the food that you eat, your friends and your family? What type of job are you doing?

What are some of the activities that you are doing? Do you travel and if so where to? Where do you live? What are your finances like?

_____

_____

_____

_____

_____

_____

_____

_____

_____

_____

_____

_____

_____

_____

_____

_____

_____

_____

_____

_____

_____

_____

_____

_____

_____

_____

_____

_____

_____

_____

_____

By having a clear understanding of who your ideal self would be and what type of life you would be living, you have the opportunity to use the exercises outlined above to help you use the power of your thoughts to support you in becoming this person. I suggest you write out a description of your ideal self and ideal life, first as it would look ten years from today, then five years, then two years and then just one year from today. By doing this you will begin to essentially set goals for yourself and your life. By starting at the furthest point – ten years from today – it is easier for your mind to imagine what you truly want without ED's commentary, because there is so much time in between. Then by asking yourself, "Well if this is what I want in ten years, then where would I have to be in five years and then two years and one year?" you can begin to envision your ideal self and ideal life as they come to life. It is often easier to set intentions for our ideals selves when we think about what we would want our future to look like, if anything was possible and there were no restrictions.

Once you can get your thoughts in alignment with the person you would like to be, alongside connecting back to activities and interests that you enjoyed as a child, teenager and young adult, you will begin to try out new behaviors and ways of being that are separate from ED. For it is through this process of actually adopting new behaviors, actions and ways of being that you begin to live your life separate from ED.

As you begin to adopt these new behaviors, watch how all the other parts of your ideal life start coming to you. Again, this takes time, dedication, commitment, belief and persistence in quieting down all of ED's doubts.

(8) Vision Boards

Another useful exercise that you can try out in hopes of not only creating a separation from ED, but beginning to rediscover who you already were and creating who you would like to be is through making a Vision Board. For those of you that are not familiar with what Vision Boards are, they are simply just a piece of paper filled with images, phrases, quotes and anything else that you want to bring into your life and that inspires you.

I suggest that you use a Bristol board to make your Vision Board out of. Cut out magazine pictures, find quotes that you love and add anything that you want to attract and bring into your life onto this board. For example, maybe one day you want to go travelling. I would suggest putting the places you would like to go to on this board. Maybe you want to find comfort in your skin. I would suggest putting a picture of someone you feel exudes this feeling or a quote that says, "I love the skin I am in." With that being said you can take any or all of your Positive Affirmations that you made earlier and put them on your board.

Essentially there is no right or wrong way to make a Vision Board, all that matters is that you do it!

Remember you do not need to know how whatever you want will happen. That is not the goal of this board. Nor is the goal to make you feel bad about yourself that you haven't achieved those dreams, goals, hopes and desires yet. A Vision Board is another means for you to focus on what you want to bring into your life rather than think about all the things that aren't currently working.

I suggest that you put your Vision Board somewhere in your room so you can look at it each day. When you look at it try to feel what it would feel like if whatever you put on the board came true. The most important thing about creating and using a Vision Board daily is to have fun with it. This is an opportunity for you to take everything that you have learned about yourself and your life so far and transfer it into a creative visual representation. Even if something feels silly or completely unrealistic to you, I suggest you put it on the board anyways.

This is an opportunity for you to once again break free from ED's fearful based thoughts and just connect with what you really want and who you really are. Use this board as a means to truly fall in love with yourself, your body and your life, by simply believing that you can.

I hope by this point that you are beginning to understand how creating separation from ED is not only highly important, but plausible. Now that you have begun to gain this separation from ED you may be asking yourself, "What is that part of me that is able to hear ED?" Well that part is actually your authentic self, essentially who you really are. This part of you may have been quiet for a long time, as ED's voice and opinions oftentimes take over. Don't worry if you are unsure of who this part of yourself is, or that it feels uncomfortable or unfamiliar. In the following section we will focus on awakening your authentic self, the part of you that you were really connected to when you were a child.

Before we get into the recap, I want to share a journal entry with you that I feel sums up a lot of what I spoke about in this section such as, gaining separation from ED, the healing crisis and discovering that the person that you look up to and want to be already lives inside of you.

*

January 27.2008

I still find ED creeping up, telling me lies like he used to do in the past when he would try to convince me that I was a loser and was wasting my time trying to get better. Rather than listening to what he had to say, I asked Paula where are you, where are you, where are you....? You will find the more you do this, the faster ED will leave and you will appear.

At first it may not work, because ED will try to convince you that this is ridiculous and that he is you. HE'S NOT YOU! No one on this planet was born hating themselves. No one is born with the desire to to be the worst they can be. No one dreams and hopes of becoming self-destructive. That's just ED trying to manipulate you again. Once you realize this and start to actually believe it, you – the true you – will begin to show up. Try it!

This certainly works for me now. But when I first started differentiating ED's voice from my own, the battle between the two of us left me confused, tired, scared, anxious, worried and confused some more.

I would ask my therapist, are you sure that isn't me? How do I know that that really isn't me? Maybe I am a pathetic piece of crap who doesn't deserve to be anything except miserable. But she made me realize that that wasn't me at all that's just ED talking, and he had become so entrenched in my mind that it was hard for me to differentiate that I wasn't him.

This is where the whole idea that you can be whoever you want to be comes into play. ED certainly was who I was trying to be and live for in my past. I was fighting him in my present. I sure as hell didn't want to be him in my future, I knew that much. I knew I wasn't living the life I dreamed of having when I was a child. I knew that if I couldn't get ED out of my life I was only going to cause more self-destruction and end up a miserable confused mess.

So I kept fighting. I kept hurting myself too. I kept crying and asking my therapist how many more times I was going to do this to myself until I finally realized that I was crying for a reason. I was crying because I wasn't being me. Because I was simply testing myself, with the assistance of ED to see if I could be someone who liked being self-destructive, who enjoyed hating themselves. That's not the girl I dream of being. That person sounds absolutely ridiculous; why would I want to be her?

So I fought a little more. I pushed a little farther, I searched a little bit deeper into MYSELF without ED. You know who I found? – the girl I always wished I could be. Confident. Independent. Articulate. Motivated. Powerful. Happy. Carefree. She was in me all along but was covered by ED's loud voice. I can't believe it. All this time I was hoping to be this girl I dreamed of being and she was actually me covered with garbage, broken bottles and loads of trash.

Who do you want to be? What's stopping you from being that person? Now that you know that you REALLY are this person who is hidden underneath all of your baggage how does that make you feel? Are you hopeful that you will one day be this person? Why or why not? Are you currently fighting ED too? What made you fight him, what made you want a better life for yourself?

These are important questions that individuals need to ask themselves of the road to recovery. Your past should remain in the past and your present should correlate to how you see your future.

I know this is a lot to take in right now. I know you wish that you could wake up tomorrow and have all this stuff gone and start fresh, but trust me if you work at this, really get to the root of why ED came into your life to begin with, your road to rediscovery will begin as your road of recovery is soon ending.

You sometimes need to get worse in order to get better.

*

Recap:
By beginning to separate from ED you are able to become the observer of his language and *CHOOSE* to create your own language that is in alignment with allowing you to fall in love with yourself, your body and your life. By learning how to step into the observer role, you are able to connect with your true self and not allow ED to automatically make decisions for you. When you begin to separate yourself from ED, you begin to realize that you truly are perfect just as you are.

(1) I AM AWESOME EXERCISE!

You have now just finished Section B of Part Two of this book!

Before we continue, I want to acknowledge you and tell you that you should be REALLY proud of yourself! You should know the drill by now! Before we move onto the next section I really want you to take this moment to recognize all of the great work you just did again!

Now tell yourself, "I am awesome!" Say it twice more and really believe it!

(2) I LOVE MYSELF EXERCISE!

Just like we did above, I would like you to say out loud to yourself, "I love myself." Say it twice more and really believe it!

Now I would like you to list 2 reasons why you love yourself.

"I love myself because _____

_____
_____ "

"I love myself because _____
_____
_____ "

Again, I feel that learning how to acknowledge ourselves by taking a moment and really recognizing the progress we have made is an important step in building our confidence in ourselves and our abilities. You can even take this exercise a step further by rewarding yourself with something you really love. (i.e. Your favorite latte at a coffee shop, a warm bubble bath, a nice walk by the water or a new journal). Just make sure you *CHOOSE* something that allows you to acknowledge the steps you have taken towards creating the life of your dreams.

I stare out into the water and take a deep breath in. I am amazed. I am content. I am happier than I ever believed was possible. I am completely and entirely present. I listen to the wind soar. I watch the giant waves crash into one another. I could do this for hours.

I take a deep breathe in. SSSSS Inhale, I feel my lungs and stomach fill up with fresh Australian sea air. HAAAHH Exhale, I feel all the still air inside of my body be released out through my mouth. I am instantly brought back to my childhood. The freedom that I experienced while running through the sandy shores back at my cousins cottage, diving deep into the Georgian Bay waters, is exactly what I am experiencing now. Even though I am literally on the other side of the world, I am home. I am myself. I am free. I can't believe I am here.

I grab hold of my towel and sit on the sand. My feet are placed firmly on the ground, with my knees bent in and my arms are hugging them in tightly toward my body. SSSSSS Inhale. HHAAAA Exhale. I wonder how I was ever gone for so long. I wonder how I ever left this place. I wonder why it has taken me so long to come back. I know the answer to all of my own questions: ED.

I then feel the urge, the urge I often feel, especially

in times when I am thinking about the past. I need to write. There is something inside of me that wants to be put onto paper, as it wants to be eliminated from my being. I grab hold of my journal, which ironically has a fairy on the cover sitting in the exact same position that I am currently sitting in. I smile and I open up to a fresh page. I take one more look at the water. SSSSS Inhale. HAAAA Exhale. I pop off the lid of my pen, point the pen straight down and I begin...

February 19.2009

Stepping onto the shores of Australian sand I am filled with contentment inside. ED is nowhere to be found. No words about my bathing suit body, how everyone on the beach must have been thinking such horrible and nasty things about me and the way I looked, only because now I do not think this way about myself. It has been over a year and a half since the last time I was on a beach, where others could really see my body. Where the conversations in my mind were filled with pollution and utter crap filtered straight through Ed. All I hear now is the beating pulse of my heart. All I feel now is the love that I am feeling for myself, my body just as it is and the world around me for granting me the opportunity to see it and myself the way it was always meant to be seen. Perfect just as it is.

I close my journal and stare back at the water.

SSSSSSS Inhale. AHHHAA Exhale. I am present once again. I look down at my body and wonder how I ever thought such horrible things about it and about myself. I look back up again and with the release of that last exhale I am instantly brought back to where ED first appeared in my life when I was nine years old, yet I had no idea. Back to the time when I was no longer free. Back to the time that I was trapped; trapped inside of a giant maze which simply was my own life. I stare back at the water. SSSSS Inhale. HHAAA Exhale. With the release of that exhale, I am present once again. I am still sitting on that beach, staring out into the beautiful Pacific Ocean off the east coast of Australia. As I stare farther and farther out until the ocean, I am brought back to the beginning, back to where it originally started. Back to a time when I was truly free. Back to a time that I truly was myself. I look at the water and smile. My connection to nature, most specifically the water, always allows me to find my way back to myself, as it centers me and grounds me like nothing else. The water reminds me of who I am and how I was never actually gone, I was always there, just disconnected from myself for a while and replaced by ED. Yet, in this moment I choose to see myself. In this moment I choose to feel freedom. In this moment, I choose to trust, accept, love and know myself for exactly who I am.

*

Through gaining awareness of ED and separating from him we have the opportunity to re-connect with that part of ourselves that existed inside of us when were little girls. The part of ourselves that did not care how much we weighed, how many calories we ate, how many calories we burned or the size of our pants. The part of ourselves that looked into the mirror, and not only accepted what we saw, but loved every ounce of it.

Yet, how do we re-connect with something that we have been so disconnected from for years? When we live in a world that promotes that we stay disconnected from this part of ourselves and focus on what we "should" look like and who we "should" act like. This last section will introduce you to somebody you used to know quite well, your authentic self, the person you were meant to be in this world.

Section C
Awakening Your Authentic Self

"Do not dwell in the past, do not dream of the future, concentrate the mind on the present moment."
– Buddha

Now that you have started to create a separation from ED you may be wondering who this true self of yours even is. Oftentimes we get so used to living our lives through ED's direction that when we begin to separate ourselves from him, we are unsure of who we are left being. In this next section, you will begin to awaken your authentic self that lives inside of you, while also continuing to learn how to CHOOSE a life free from ED. It is through this process that you will truly begin to fall in love with yourself, your body and your life like you always dreamed was possible.

(1) From DOING to BEING: Learning How To Live In The Present Moment

During the course of this entire book I have presented numerous questions and exercises for you to *do* in order for you to create a life separate from ED. You have learned the importance of cleaning up your *past* and the value that there is in writing out ideas around the person you would like to be in your *future*. Though both of these things are highly important in learning how to be in love with yourself, your body and your life, this does, however, leave out one very essential and important part of your life, the *present* moment.

At the end of the day all we truly have any real *CHOICE* over is the present moment. It is through learning how to be still, learning how to truly connect with what you have today and where you are in this exact moment that allows you to experience life the way that you always dreamed was possible.

The reason why I have waited this long to introduce this concept to you is because unless and until you can begin to separate from ED, learning how to connect to the present moment is quite challenging. Even with all of this knowledge of ED in mind, learning how to be still and accept the present moment for what it is, is a lot easier said than done.

In the next section you will find three simple exercises that you can start today to help you begin to connect with the present moment through learning how to just *be*. Before I get into the exercises I wanted to share a journal entry with you that I wrote about during my travels after I finished university.

February 26.2009

Learning how to accept myself and my current place in life by not having to specifically be doing anything is such a change for me. Not defining myself according to the situation around me. Not labeling myself as anything this year (since school ended) has been a necessity in my life as up until this past year I have always had some sort of status – i.e. student – to define who I was in this world, I also do not have a secure plan to what I am actually coming home to, which I again believe is a necessity for me.

There are times during particular days where my natural tendencies creep up. Anxiety. Wanting to plan or control things a particular way, all in attempts to try to make up for the fact that I am actually not really 'doing' much right now, even though I am. Travelling the last three weeks has been very much related to what I would have done at home, yet not having a job is what is missing. Overall, in attempting to teach myself that I am perfect just as I currently am, as are all people, I too am teaching myself that what I am doing at any particular moment, even if it is simply being still, is perfect as well.

*

(2) From DOING to BEING Exercises

(A) Shower Exercise

The shower holds a perfect opportunity for you to connect with the present moment. Oftentimes people take daily showers without even really being aware that they did. What I mean by this is because ED is so used to telling you what you are going to do after you get out of the shower, reminding you to think about things that happened to you earlier in your day, or things that happened to you in the past, you can get in and out of the shower without even feeling that you got wet. The goal of this exercise is for you to actually feel the water on your skin. This is another opportunity for you to quiet ED and connect with the present moment where you are able to feel the water on your skin.

Just like with the exercises I gave you earlier in regards to the mindset gym, you once again have the opportunity to work out your mind with this exercise. The reason why I chose the shower as a place for you to practice being present is because it is something we all do that doesn't take up too much time and also gives us privacy to focus on this exercise.

The next time you are in the shower I want you to

focus on feeling the water that is pouring on your skin. Do you feel the water in your hair when you are washing it? Do you feel the water on your back, your legs, your arms, your face? ED may show up to try to take you out of the present moment and cause you to think about other things, but I want you to try again to connect back to that feeling, to the water. This is certainly going to take practice but as mentioned above this is a great place to start being present.

Once you have learned how to just *be* in the shower, I invite you to take this same type of exercise, which focuses on what you're actually doing, and use it in other areas of your life (i.e. driving, walking down the street.)

(B) Breathing Exercise

Our breath is an amazing gift that we have been granted with that keeps us alive. Yet, for many of us we are not even aware that we are breathing, let alone ever purposely try to focus on it. However, when we do focus on our breath, we not only have an opportunity to allow it to slow down our nervous system, allow our mind to calm down and cause us to de-stress, but it also allows us to connect with the present moment.

The goal of this exercise is for you to focus on and

connect with your breath. This is another opportunity for you to quiet ED and connect with the present moment through allowing your breath to guide you.

For this exercise, I would like you to lie down in a comfortable position and location. If you have a yoga mat, you can lay that down on the ground in your room or you can even lie on your bed. Regardless of what you *CHOOSE*, I want you to close your eyes and put one hand on your chest and the other hand on your stomach. With each inhalation, feel your chest expand. With every exhalation, feel it drop.

Continue to do this while you take deep inhalations through your nose and out through your mouth. I suggest that you do this exercise as many times a day as you are able, even just for two-minute intervals. This is also an excellent thing to do every night before you go to bed and every morning for at least five minutes.

This too is going to take practice but it is also a simple way to start learning how to just *be*. I invite you to take this newfound knowledge of the power of connecting to your breath and use it in other parts of your day. Begin to watch how you not only are able to connect with your breath and your body, lower your stress levels, but also heighten your connection with the present moment.

(C) Nature Exercise

Being in nature is an amazing way to practice just being still and connecting with the present moment. Seeing the beauty in nature as the wind blows through the trees or watching the ducks gently float on top of the water without ED's commentary distracting you and ultimately taking you out of that present moment are two perfect examples of how you can do this.

I invite you to go in nature as often as you are able, even if for just five minutes a day, and connect with a piece of wildlife such trees, clouds, stars, or birds. What I mean by connect, is begin to focus your senses on them, while allowing ED to quiet his thoughts, and just *be* with whatever you are focusing on.

I believe that nature, especially animals, have a lot of lessons to teach us about our existence on this planet if we can just *be* still with it for a while. In this next journal entry you can begin to see what I mean about using nature as a way for you to connect with the present moment and accepting it for exactly what it is.

*

March 19.2009
And the Rooster Crows – I'm home!
I opened my eyes from an interesting night's sleep and
knew I was in Bali, Indonesia. Oh my God, reading about
this in Eat. Pray. Love...I never would have imagined
that only a half of a year later I would be sitting here.

As Kyla and I headed outdoors from our cute little place
my eyes were in shock of the magazine scene that was
waiting for us. The wildlife here is completely incredible!
Greens have never looked so green, birds have never soared
so freely and the sound of chickens, roosters, birds, bugs,
frogs and more is so amazing I cannot even believe that
my ears are fortunate to hear it all and my eyes are able
to see what I am seeing!

When Kyla and I arrived late last night a man from the
Yoga school we were going to was waiting to take us to
Ubud. He was very friendly and sweet, trying to speaking
English and tell us street names, city names, festivals and
so on. We got in the car, where they drive on the other side
of the road and headed out for our over one hour drive
from Denpassar to Ubud.

About five minutes into this drive I already noticed a few
things. The way they drive here is quite different than
back home. Passing other cars by going on the other side

of the road (like we normally do in cottage country) was normal; driving in the middle of two lanes seemed like a natural thing. Almost hitting the hundreds of people on motorcycles was as natural as anything could be, but for some reason it all works out, nobody got angry, not our driver or anyone else; that's just how it was!

I also noticed that they had MANY huge signs posted all over their streets. Many seemed like political stuff, however, there were also massive signs announcing just about anything. Dogs roaming freely, people off to the side, all of these things were so amazing to see. This morning I had a thought, that somewhat sprung up yesterday on the plane to come here. I feel like I am in chapter two of my life. I know spending the next few months in Asia is just where I am supposed to be.

Being in South East Asia, I feel like I am somewhat at home here, where I belong right now as I drink my tea, write in my journal and listen to the roosters crow again and again. I just had a thought; I got such a good fix of beaches over the last month, the water was absolutely amazing up the east coast of Australia, but I am ready for more, different cultures, different wildlife, I want greens, I want animals, and look where I am!

As the ducks waddled across the watery greens I notice the beauty in their waddle, the uniqueness as that not all creatures are able to move and do what they are able to. The birds soar above their heads looking for a place to land their little feet. The baby cries as it longs for something which most adults have no idea what that is. The roosters crow to make themselves be heard, to allow others to know they are there.

As I wrote this about 60 ducks came waddling out, all running towards one another, following in a line all in attempts to cool themselves off between the watery greens. As they walk ahead to the swampy land, their beaks are in the mud probably finding their tasty breakfast that is hidden under the soil. That is how they spend their morning hours, in unison with one another, all attempts of reaching the same goal. I saw no arguing, no fighting, no pushing or shoving to get ahead of their cousins, brothers or sisters, friends or neighbors, I just saw pure love and natural behavior. Watching the ducks this morning taught me so much, it showed me how individuals in our human world could connect and live with one another, could interact, could get along. It also showed me the beauty that lies within each and every creature on this planet and what comes along with each unique ability each one possesses.

I know I am going to write many books! Ahh!! If this trip has taught me anything it is this. I love to write, I need to write, this is who I am and I am learning that more and more each day. I think what I wrote above could be called the beginning of Chapter Two. I am not sure what exactly that book will be about but its more about awakening and living life from a place filled with stillness, being present and soaking up each breath, each visual perception, each auditory sound.

I want to focus on the perceptual sensory elements we all have, the five senses and how we become extremely habituated to what we are presented with each day; even now my eyes and ears over the course of an hour have become somewhat accustomed to this magnificent sight, the initial sense of love and joy I experienced when I first looked is not there.

I believe this occurs in all areas of life, including relationships, what you possess naturally and so on because our mind and our EGOS trick us unto believing we need more.

Okay that's beautiful and I get it but what next? What else can I see? Seeing or hearing the beauty that lies within that very same scene is very easy to experience if you first allow yourself to be still, be present and breathe in. When you do all of these things the connection to the beauty that you first experienced when you looked out at that scene reappears. The feeling I get while sitting here is freedom as these animals are able to express themselves as they wish with acceptance of who they are. Meaning this is what they do. None of them are trying to crow like the rooster or swing from the trees like a monkey. They are simply happy and content with themselves and all they are able to do. Why is it that humans have such a hard time experiencing or reaching this state of authentic happiness? Authentic expression?

*

By learning the power of living your life in the present moment where you are going from a place of *DOING* to *BEING*, you begin to further disconnect from ED's influential and demanding ideas around who you are. When I speak of the word *DOING*, I am referring to the fact that ED always causes us to feel as though we need to be *DOING* something, as *BEING* still is either a *waste of time,* means *you should be DOING something else,* means *you are lazy,* means *you are not good enough,* or means *you are not worthy.*

The truth of the matter is that the reason why ED says all of this stuff to you is because according to him, who you are as a person is defined by what you *DO* compared to *who you just are*. This has been conditioned as a result of the way in which our society is set up, where people automatically ask one another things such as, *What do you DO for a living? What did you DO today? What are you going to DO this weekend? What are you DOING for your birthday.* It is through this notion that individuals are supposed to always be *DOING* things that we oftentimes have an extremely difficult time just *BEING* without feeling highly uncomfortable or guilty, as if we are doing something wrong. Yet, truly loving yourself, your body and your life can only occur when you love yourself enough to *be* still, *be* quiet, *DO* nothing and relax your mind. Through quieting the mind, which is ED, and learning how to just *be* still through connecting with the present moment, you have the ability to truly awaken your authentic self.

Recap:
All we truly have *CHOICE* over is the present moment. By gaining awareness and separation from ED you are able to connect with the present moment much more easily. Focusing on the water of your daily shower, your breath and being in nature are three great ways to connect to the present moment and quiet your mind. By learning how to live your life from a place *BEING* rather than *DOING* you begin to connect with your authentic self.

(3) You Are On A Journey Of Transformation

You have just been introduced to the enormous power that there is in learning how to *be* still and connect with the present moment. In order to be automatically connected with the present moment, know that this is something that is going to take practice, as ED has been so good at causing you to escape from the present moment for years.

I would like to be crystal clear that this process of learning how to connect with your true self and the present moment, does not simply mean that ED is never going to be the one who is making your choices, actions, thought process and behaviors from here on out. ED is not "bad", "good", "right" or "wrong" – he just is what he is, our EGO.

I remember when I first started going through this process I would get mad and disappointed at myself when I knew ED was the one still in control, calling myself weak or feeling like I would never change and ED would always win. The truth of the matter is that way of thinking is completely false.

Think of it this way: you have been thinking and acting the way that you have been for as many years as you have been alive. How can you expect that in the matter of a day, week, month or even a year that everything in your life is going to be entirely different? If you think this way you are approaching this whole process through ED once again, which is situated in judgment, expectation, rules, guidelines and fear.

There is usually an unrealistic expectation associated with gaining separation from ED, in that you are to follow this straight line that will lead you from one place to the next, ultimately veering you away from ED. This way of thinking couldn't be anything further from the truth. When you are living with an ED who is also an Eating Disorder, this is even more apparent since ED has unrealistic expectations about everything. He always places his expectations higher than human's can ever truthfully attain. He expects perfection in everything and ridicules and judges when that doesn't automatically occur.

As mentioned earlier, the truth is that when you are on the path of gaining separation from ED and ultimately beginning to awaken your authentic self, a straight and narrow line is nowhere in sight.

Rather, there is a winding road that leads you forward then back, left then right, up then down. Though you are heading in the direction of obtaining the original intention that you stated at the beginning of this book, which ultimately is about falling in love with yourself, your body and your life, it is important to know that you will not always feel like you are going in that direction. I want you to know that not only is this completely and entirely normal, but it is expected in this process, regardless of what ED may say.

When you are going through this process, which I like to call a ***journey of transformation***, having *understanding, love, compassion, patience* and *forgiveness* towards yourself during this time is very essential. Using the notion of connecting to the present moment and learning how to just *be* can also assist you in this process as well.

The reason why I call this process a ***journey of transformation*** is because when you are working on gaining awareness and then separation from ED, you truly are transforming yourself. The word *transformation* refers to the notion that you are living a life that was directed by ED and transforming it into a life that is *CHOSEN* by the real you. As you begin to transform yourself, you simultaneously awaken your authentic self. The word *journey* represents the notion that this is something that is not going to happen overnight, where you are travelling in a sense, from one place to another. Again this journey is not a straight and narrow path but rather a winding road.

Some individuals react to this notion of *transformation* by interpreting it to represent a challenge that is going to take way too long to attain. I believe that people respond and react this way because we live in a society that claims that there are quick fixes for pretty much any and everything. Some examples of this are: if your head hurts you take a pill. If you want to lose weight follow this diet or take a diet pill. If you don't have any money, you use your credit card and you can get what you want right then and there.

If you think about it pretty much everything that bothers us or causes hassle to our lives has some sort of quick and easy solution available. Living in a society that is set up like this results in the belief that anything that causes us pain, discomfort, hassle or annoyance has a quick and easy solution readily available. By interpreting things in this way it automatically sets us up for not valuing and understanding this *journey of transformation* that I am speaking of and further disconnects us from our true selves. For it is oftentimes the things that we label as pain, discomfort, annoyance and hassle that actually hold enormous power in connecting us with our authentic selves. This next sub-section will address just that.

(A) How Our Feelings & Emotions Play A Role In Our Journey Of Transformation

Earlier in this book, I already spoke about the enormous power that our thoughts have in directing our lives in the manner we would like it to go. While it is quite essential to work on your thoughts and *CHOOSE* to speak a different language completely separate from ED, it is also highly important to learn how to understand your feelings and emotions.

When we are used to living with ED as the director of our lives, he oftentimes does not allow us to experience any negative emotions, as they do not make us feel good. Yet, when you are in the process of awakening your authentic self, one very important part of this is connecting with your emotions, identified as both pleasant and unpleasant feelings.

Some feelings can make us uncomfortable, as we are often unable to understand them and process them for what they are. Many people have a difficult time associating with their feelings as well as allowing their feelings to play out. As I mentioned earlier, different means such as food, alcohol, or even watching television are often used to cope with uncomfortable feelings like sadness or anxiety. Choosing external stimuli that serve as a resource to alter the current state of one's feelings is quite normal.

Distraction, numbness or avoidance of these feelings plays an enormous role in helping us be able to cope with whatever it is that we are going through.

However, doing so does not always serve our best interests. Continually disregarding our feelings results in a disconnection from our authentic selves, hence why when we are in the process of awakening our authentic self our feelings play an enormous role. Our feelings occur for a reason, oftentimes to tell us something we are unable to see through our psyche. By cutting off the connection to our true feelings we in turn allow ED to take more control of our lives. As we have learned, ED doesn't necessarily have our best interests at heart. ED shows up in times of fear and discomfort and cleverly creates reasoning or excuses as to why things are okay or not okay.

When you *CHOOSE* to tune into your feelings rather than checkout through external stimuli, which is often facilitated by ED, an opportunity to grow and connect with your authentic self is presented. Though it may feel uncomfortable and unfamiliar, the best thing you can do with new feelings that you are not sure how to process is to just *be* still and sit with them.

By actually acknowledging your feelings for what they are and experiencing them as a part of your life rather than trying to avoid or numb them through external stimuli you will begin to develop a deeper understanding of yourself. Your feelings serve as very powerful tools for self-awareness as they are associated and connected to a deeper part of yourself that we are usually not taught to give any validity to. This lack of belief around our feelings serving a deeper purpose and connection to our authentic selves is usually disregarded in our society.

This notion can be seen when we feel sad, anxious or depressed and we go to our doctors for help. We are typically given pharmaceutical drugs to serve as a quick and easy solution to avoid these uncomfortable and painful feelings and emotions. I am not here to bash pharmaceutical drugs or to claim that all situations are the same, because I realize each case is based on the individual's experience, biochemistry, genetics and more. What I am here to say though is that oftentimes individuals experience these uncomfortable feelings and emotions as a way for a part of ourselves, which we may not be highly connected with, to communicate with us. The same can be said about the way in which we treat physical symptoms that arise throughout our body, such as gastrointestinal discomfort. We go to the doctor and once again we receive medication to alleviate the pain. We can also just simply go to the drug store and grab something off the counter that stops the pain.

Nowhere in any of these examples that I have presented has the question, *"Why have these feelings, emotions and/or physical symptoms presented them-selves?"* been asked.

Again, I am not here to bash pharmaceutical drugs or medication as I acknowledge and recognize that they play an important role in particular people's lives. Yet, as a result of living in a society where we are taught that pain and uncomfortable feelings are bad and we need to get rid of them immediately, we miss out on opportunities to really learn about the reasons why we are experiencing this pain or discomfort to begin with. This is not to disregard that we do have a *physical body* that oftentimes does experience pain solely as a result of a physical ailment. Our society is very accepting and accommodating of these types of symp-toms and oftentimes only sees the *physical body* as the main or entire source to be healed. Yet, this is not always the case as we are made up of more than just our *physical body*.

As a result of being unable to process the thoughts, feelings and emotions that we are experiencing, as we have become so good at shoving them under the rug or hiding them behind the closet, our bod-ies oftentimes have no other way of trying to release them but through manifesting themselves as physical symptoms. Since they show up as physical symptoms, this often causes individuals to not only ignore, but be completely ignorant of the enormous value that our *mental body* and *emotional body* play in causing these symptoms and feelings to arise in our lives. Furthermore, we may experience these uncomfortable feelings or symptoms as a means of our *spiritual body* trying to communicate with us as well. You may have just been thrown off by the mentioning of the term *spiritual body*, but the truth of the matter is that we all have a spirit within us, as we are much more than just *physical*, *emotional* and *mental* beings.

(B) How Our Spiritual Body Is Highly Connected With Our Authentic Selves

Our spirit is the thing inside of us that is in direct connection to our authentic self, highly influences and guides our intuitions and sees ED, our EGOS, for what they truly are – fear. In the last sub-section I spoke about the enormous value that our feelings and emotions have in our *journey of transformation*. It is important to recognize that ED is founded in fear while our authentic self is founded in love.

Many emotions such as *anxiety, depression, guilt, resentment, hate, revenge, anger, worry and shame* sit on top of fear, while feelings such as *gratitude, joy, hope, happiness, passion* and *satisfaction* sit on top of love. With this knowledge in mind, you can experience your spirit connecting with your authentic self when you feel complete *satisfaction* when you are looking out at the ocean, when you feel *gratitude* when you look at nature, when you feel *happiness* when you look at a newborn baby and when you feel pure *joy* when you truly love another human being and/or yourself. This is the part of you that I was guiding you to reach and connect with, by learning how to *be* still in the present moment.

When we are truly present we are able to connect with this part of ourselves. When you are living a life where which ED is in the forefront, your spirit has become so suppressed that you have disconnected from it. This is why it is often more challenging or difficult to experience loving types of emotions for a long period of time, as ED usually shows up and distracts us from these feelings. The point of this is not to place judgment or criticism on the fact that this disconnection took place, as I believe this is part of the purpose of life in a sense – to disconnect, to struggle, to feel pain, to learn from these experiences and to begin to awaken our authentic selves, which is connected to our spirit. However, as a result of living in this world and being raised by numerous adults who are also conditioned by ED and disconnected from their spirits, your *spiritual body* has a more challenging time communicating with and to your authentic self. This is where the notion of your intuition plays an important role in connecting with your authentic self.

*

July 2.2011
The rain is falling so lightly its sound has become so peaceful to me. I am alone again in my Vancouver bedroom. The beauty that Vancouver holds is so amazing, words cannot describe the pleasure my eyes experienced earlier today, not to mention my soul. The sparkling water, the countless white sailboats, the mountains, the ocean, it was the most beautiful scene I could have ever asked to see.

I never used to think about the mountains, why would I? I never really ever saw them before moving here. Their enormous space and force is so ridiculous, you can't help but be grounded and really see the beauty that is on our planet earth. We, as a North America society specifically, are so disconnected from this earth, from who we are, just beings, organisms, life forces, spiritual beings – whatever you want to call us and that we are not the center of the universe but rather a little part of it. I think when humans forget that and no longer see the bigger picture of life itself, our planet and furthermore our universe, we are not living form our soul, our spirit, but rather from our mind, as we conform to what is told to us, which as we know by looking at history changes year after year, decade after decade.

Learning to be present in the moment and seeing it for what it is, how to allow all these deep, very intuitive and perceptive, not to mention curious thoughts about our existence on this planet is something I am working on as different parts of myself unfold: partly socializer, partly loner, philosopher, psychologist, counselor, dancer, life coach, friend, sister, daughter, and so much more – I question myself more and more. Who am I really? And is that a question that can ever actually be answered? I am torn by feeling that no, it cannot be answered and then yes it can be, because who I am is who I choose to be at that moment, but oftentimes I do things to surprise myself and it makes me question who I believe I was.

Crazy, how much I have changed and continue to change. If I could sum up the growth I experienced recently the proper word is acceptance. I am not attached to anything like I used to be, which is the working of the EGO/ED driven mind. Being in the space of acceptance is very liberating, especially for me because I often live in fantasy land, wanting to escape reality because I was unable to accept myself, accept my family, accept my sister, accept my friends, accept Etobicoke, accept Toronto, accept Canada and more. I wasn't able to accept any of it for what it was and be okay with it.

Without acceptance comes a need to control. Control others to be who you expect them to be, control yourself to act a certain perfect way. Control it all – ED. When you accept there is no place for a need to control you then live in a space of complete freedom because you are not attached to anything. There is nothing holding you onto something; I guess that's what people mean when they talk about letting go

I feel the spirit in me start to change, to grow, to get excited. Something inside of me says, keep doing what you are doing and you are going to have this amazing life you always dream about. I believe it, as I believe in that voice because I know it's spirit. It is the part of me that knows best, the part that knows I am following the right path for my human existence to unfold as it should.

*

Recap:
The process of gaining awareness of ED, separating from ED and then awakening your authentic self can be seen as a *Journey of Transformation*. Our feelings and emotions play an enormous part in allowing us to understand this journey a bit better. By understanding that we are made up of more than just *physical, mental* and *emotional bodies*, we can begin to recog-

nize the enormous value that our *spiritual bodies* play in the role of connecting us with our authentic selves.

(4) The Importance Of Recognizing Your Intuition

Our intuition, also referred to as our gut, is a part of ourselves that I believe can be accessed at all times in our lives. It is that part of ourselves that we often second guess as ED has convinced us to believe that what he thinks is the truth.

When individuals are creating a separation from ED, learning how to be guided by their intuition is often easier, as ED's language is not playing on automatic anymore.

I wanted to address this point because when we are in the process of awakening our authentic selves, our intuition plays an enormous role. Since our intuition is the place of inner wisdom and knowledge, as it is influenced and guided by spirit, learning how to respond to its direction even when ED may disagree is highly valuable.

One big thing I find challenging for people when they are first learning how to live a life separate from ED and listening to their intuition, comes from a lack of trust. When I speak of trust, I am referring to two things, self-trust and trusting in the wisdom and connection that our intuitions have. As mentioned earlier, gaining self-trust was a very challenging thing for me. What was even more challenging was trusting this part of me that didn't have logical reasoning or even made sense. It was more of an internal nudge that almost guided me to where I was meant to go, what I was meant to do or where I was supposed to be.

I will be completely transparent in saying that at this exact moment that I am writing this book, in 2013, I am still working on allowing my intuition to guide me. I believe that this is going to be a work in progress, as my mind still wants to have it "all figured out." I remind myself that I can plan, control and set out intentions for what I would like to have happen, but at the end of the day I need to be able to surrender and let go when things don't necessarily go according to plan.

This is where the trust comes into play. Trust not only in myself but trust in something bigger than me, an inner wisdom that even though I don't fully understand it, I know has a connection to the world around me and to a part of life that ED thankfully will never understand.

I think of it this way, I have listened and followed ED's

suggestions and commands for so many years, but where did that get me? Certainly not to a place where I was happy, so why would I continue listening to him, when there is this other part of myself that even though I don't fully understand it, has always ended up guiding me to a place that promotes my best interest?

I hope my own experience and opinion about this has allowed you to see that when you can get past ED's controlling ways and start to truly trust, you can begin to start being guided by your intuition. You begin to connect with your feelings in a way that you might have never done before. You begin to listen to your body and become connected to what it wants or does not want and what it desires and doesn't desire. You begin to start making decisions from a place of inner knowing, versus limited rules and rigid guidelines that you *should* follow according to ED.

It is through listening to your intuition and seeing the positive results that it brings that you will begin to feel less inclined to listen to ED again. It is through listening to your intuition that you begin to feel what the true sense of freedom means, living a life where you are truly the one making the *CHOICE* in everything you do. I invite you to trust in this gut feeling and watch how your life begins to change enormously.

Since we are on the topic of learning to be guided by your intuition and this book talks about learning how to fall in love with yourself, your body and your life, I briefly want to talk about the concept of Intuitive Eating. I could write an entire book about this, but I thought it was a very valuable piece to add to the concept of falling in love with your body.

(A) The Power of Intuitive Eating

As I mentioned earlier, listening to our intuition comes from a place that is completely separated from ED. With this in mind, when you hear the term, *Intuitive Eating* you can think of it as learning how to eat without the involvement of EDs input and language.

That means there are no "bad" or "good" foods, no calorie counting, and no, *"I messed up today, so I will just start eating perfectly tomorrow, or on Monday or the beginning of next month."*

Without having ED dictate your dynamic with food, you have the opportunity to allow your relationship with food to develop into something positive, one that is stemming from a place of love. What I mean by this is no longer does food need to be seen through the lens of ED's rigid rules that often label food in an all or nothing mentality that can keep many people captive. Rather, food can become something that you *CHOOSE* to ingest as nutrition for your body and pleasure for your taste buds. The way you see food can transform into something that you are now positively connected with.

Learning how to intuitively eat, however, takes a lot of awareness through teaching your mind to be still. It results in allowing your body to ask for what it yearns for and stopping to eat when it no longer feels it needs food.

I wanted to briefly present this topic because it is something that I believe is the real and only way to truly find freedom with food. Finding freedom with food does not ignore the importance of nutrition, however. Eating a diet filled with healthy fats, proteins, complex carbs, vitamins and minerals is highly important for obtaining optimal health and wellbeing. Depending on your educational level in this area you may need help from a nutritionist and/or books to ensure that you are eating all of these types of foods daily.

Yet, it is important to note that when you are learning how to intuitively eat, you do not want to get wrapped up in black and white thinking. The goal in learning how to intuitively eat is not about setting up a plan and getting it perfect and "right". It's not about learning more content. Even the most educated individuals in nutrition can still have Eating Disorders or Disordered Eating patterns in their life. Learning how to intuitively eat doesn't come from feeding your mind with more information. It is about gently combining your educational knowledge around nutrition with your intuitive instincts.

Your body is very smart and in most instances it knows what it needs. It is our responsibility to listen to it and provide it what it yearns for. It is really quite simple – if the food that you eat comes from the earth, then those foods hold the most nutritional content for your body. If humans had to process it into something else than those foods hold less nutritional content than the foods that come directly from the earth. It is not to say that one food is "good" while the other is "bad". Rather it is important to recognize that some foods have more nutritional value for our bodies than others. I do realize that eating this way is much easier said than done especially when food is used as a means to deal with emotions.

There are always individual expectations to everything and learning about intuitive eating could also be a completely separate book. In fact it will be a book, as I am currently beginning to write about this topic. For now, I just wanted to give you a taste of what your life can start to look like when you are completely separated from ED. For truly learning how to love your body comes also from learning how to fall in love with the food you eat.

- If you feel you would benefit from the support of others in trying to learn how to intuitively eat, feel free to contact me at www.paulagalli.com or go see a Holistic Nutritionist or Naturopath in your area.

With this new knowledge about your intuition, I want you to know that learning how to live your life directed solely from this place will be a work in progress. For now, I want you to become *aware* of your intuition so you can recognize the enormous value that it does hold in your life. It is through learning how to listen to your intuition that you will begin to awaken your authentic self.

Recap:
Our intuition plays an enormous role when we are in the process of awakening our authentic selves, since it is guided and influenced by our spirit. By learning to be steered by your intuitive instincts, rather than ED's demands, you will begin to connect with yourself and your body in a way that you have never done before.

This connection will allow you to do such things as eat intuitively, where you will eat food based on your body's request. The more you listen to your intuition, the easier it will be for you to connect with your authentic self.

(5) The Journey Of Transformation Truly Never Ends

In this section you have been introduced to the enormous influential power that your feelings and emotions play in your life. By briefly learning about your intuition you may have begun to see what your life would look if fear was no longer at the forefront of your every *CHOICE* and decision.

It is important to note that this *journey of transformation* that I spoke about earlier truly never ends. For when you are *CHOOSING* to no longer allow ED, which is simply just fear presenting itself, to stop you, you will always be growing, changing and transforming, while simultaneously just finding your way back to something that already exists inside of you, your authentic self.

As I mentioned at the beginning of the second half of the book, even when ED no longer stands for an Eating Disorder, as his language may change; ED will still exist as Everyone's Disorder-essentially our EGO.

I would like to reiterate this point and say the EGO, ED is not "bad", "good", "right" or "wrong", it just is what it is, and like you know now has just been formulated and conditioned by things from our past. The faster we can stop judging ED and accept it as a part of ourselves, the less of a struggle we will have in not only acknowledging his existence but in resisting this *journey of transformation* that we are on.

By accepting ED as part of ourselves, we admit to ourselves that we are simply human. You can take this a step further and say that we are all just *physical, emotional, mental* and *spiritual beings* living a human existence, where which ED is part of that experience.

Again, I am saying this to you because I remember at the beginning of my awakening – as some people like to call this, awakening in the sense that you begin to become disassociated from ED – I used to think that I would be able to live a life completely free from ED. Now this isn't to say that that is impossible, as in my opinion that is exactly what people who have reached the state of enlightenment or nirvana attain. Even though this state is not reached by many or most people it is possible if that is what someone *CHOOSES* and commits their life to achieving, but is not by any means the goal of this book. The goal is to present you with how ED's presence influences your life. It is important to know that it is in this state of truly awakening and connecting with your authentic self, where real and genuine love for yourself, your body and your life stems from. By using this simple knowledge as you are moving forward you can begin to develop the awareness around whether your *CHOICES* are stemming from a place of fear or love, which ultimately allows you to know if ED or your authentic self is at the forefront.

At the end of the day, what we truly want to obtain in our lives is freedom, happiness and love. Freedom with food, freedom from our own internal negative thoughts that are directed by ED and which in turn block us from living our dream life. For it is those things that we as human beings are all yearning for, not the perfect body or eating the perfect amount of food. Yet, for some reason we have gotten it all mixed up.

Remember you were not born into this world with any tags on you indicating how you would end up or who you had to be. You were not born being concerned with a number on the scale, the amount of calories you ate, the amount of calories you burned off or the size of your pants. You were not born being concerned with the style of your hair, the color of your nails, the purse that you carried or the car that you drove. You were not born caring if other people liked you, accepted you or wanted to be your friend. You weren't concerned about any of this because you were a beacon of love - love for yourself that is.

By now I am sure that you have learned that it is about so much more than all of that. It's truly about stepping into your inner world and transforming it into something that supports and nurtures you. It's about living your life with a positive self-TALK (self-trust, self, acceptance, self-love, self-knowledge). Once you incorporate a positive self-TALK into your everyday life, CHOOSING foods that nourish your mind, body and soul, along with being active in order to help your body do what it is meant to do – move – will occur naturally. It will stem automatically from your authentic self that is filled with love in giving yourself everything that you truly desire and deserve.

When you can begin to live your life from this place, everything around you shifts and changes, because you have truly begun to no longer weigh your love according to any external thing. You have experienced what truly loving yourself, your body and your life feels like, just like you did when you were a child.

*

October 14.2012

Accepting reality. Choosing reality. Taking in every moment of reality.

Feeling the happiness. Feeling the laughter. Feeling the joy. Feeling the pain.

Feeling the discomfort and not running away.

Feeling the uncomfortable and not numbing it through externals, through shallows.

Feeling the disappointment when things did not turn out the way that you expected, the way that you wanted.

Feeling the sadness when your heart is broken but knowing it will mend again and when it's meant to be you will fall in love again.

Feeling loneliness when it arises and knowing that you are not alone as your self is always with you.

Feeling love from others as well as yourself and knowing that you deserve all of it.

No longer do I feel any need to escape reality like I used to. Sure there are days that are tougher than others but then again I am a human being and this is what I believe is part of the journey of life.

The difference between now and before is that now I am no longer scared of reality, as I truly believe that whatever moment I am in I am meant to be there.

Accepting reality isn't always easy and for me it definitely wasn't.

However, learning how to accept reality in fact only occurs through learning how to live in the now and through learning how to be present.

Don't get me wrong, setting goals and dreams for your future is something I strongly believe in and are useful tools that moved me forward in my life but by living in your future dreams and goals you are escaping reality in yet another way, so learning to live in the present is important.

Until you love who you actually are.

Until you become your own best friend, to me there is no greater happiness out there.

*

Recap:

By learning that we all have an ED inside of us that is ultimately trying to keep us stuck, we can begin to look at our lives from a whole new lens. When you are committed to living a life in which ED or fear no longer stops you from truly falling in love with yourself, your body and your life, this *Journey Of Transformation* that we are all on, truly never ends. In this process of connecting with your authentic self, you can begin to adopt a positive self-TALK where which your everyday *CHOICES* stem from a place of *self-trust, self-acceptance, self-love* and *self-knowledge*. You in turn begin to live your life from the place you were always meant to live it from, from an abundance of love.

(1) I AM AWESOME EXERCISE!

You probably thought that I forgot about these exercises, since you haven't done them as often as you did in the other sections. Well I did not forget and actually wanted to save them for the end of this book! You just finished this book, and it is time to acknowledge that before you move onto whatever you have planned to do once you close these pages. You should know the drill by now, I want you to tell yourself, "I am awesome!" Say it twice more and really believe it!

(2) I LOVE MYSELF EXERCISE!

You just committed yourself to an intensive book that really dug deep and got you to possibly look at your life in a way that you may have never done before. I would like you to say out loud to yourself, "I love myself." Say it twice more and really believe it!

Now I would like you to list 2 reasons why you love yourself.
"I love myself because _____

_____

_____."

"I love myself because _____
_____
_____."

(3) I LOVE MY BODY EXERCISE!

Similar to the intention that I had you doing with the, "I love myself!" exercise, I would like you to say out loud to yourself, "I love my body." Say it twice more and really believe it!

Now I would like you to list 2 reasons why you love your body.
"I love my body because _____
_____
_____."
"I love my body because _____
_____
_____."

Once again, I invite you to reward yourself with something you really love, i.e. your favorite latte at a coffee shop, a warm bubble bath, a nice walk by the water or a new journal. Just make sure you *CHOOSE* something that allows you to acknowledge the fact that you just did an amazing thing by finishing this book and participating in all of the exercises.

FINAL WORDS

Before I finish writing, I feel the need to ask you to go back to your original intention of reading this book. I truly hope that this book has granted you with everything you were looking to achieve and more, or even just simply served as a place for you to start thinking about your relationship with yourself, your body and your life in a different manner.

This book has showcased some of my own journey in discovering myself for who I am, for the person I feel proud of being, for someone I know will continue to grow more each day.

I shared this story in hopes of allowing you to realize that you too can be anyone you want to be. You deserve that. You are worthy of that. You are meant to be that person. The road towards disconnecting from ED and living from your truth is not necessarily an easy road to follow. There may be bumps along the way, winding roads that try to confuse you and alternate routes you need to take in order to get to that final destination you are heading towards. Even though the final destination may have been the initial reason as to why you decided to take this drive, the sights you have seen and learned from going along the route were equally, if not more important, for you to see.

What I am trying to say is that everything you go through on this road of becoming your true self is exactly what you were meant to learn, for it is through suffering that we learn who we truly are.

I have countless dreams, wishes and goals for myself but I also have dreams, wishes and goals for you. Seeing others live their life from their truth, being their potential and not settling for anything less than they deserve excites me. Seeing people absolutely in love with themselves and their bodies for exactly who they are and what they look like is one of the most inspiring things to me.

When someone truly loves themselves, it automatically gives permission to others to do the same. I invite you to be one of those people, the ones who find comfort in their skin, the ones who accept everything about themselves, the ones who love themselves just as they would love their own child.

I invite you to stop *Weighing Love,* love for yourself that is, by the things around you or particular numbers that you think equate with perfection.

I invite you to give yourself the permission to just surrender to the beautiful and perfect being that you are, mind, body and soul, for it is that you, the authentic you, that you were meant to be in this world. She is there inside of you; all you have to do is look within and greet her with love.

Lastly, for me, there was no choice in the matter of how I ended up where I am today. Helping individuals learn to fall in love with themselves, their bodies and the food that they eat is my requirement and is my purpose. I chose this yes, but on some level I feel like it has been chosen for me.

Because I truly care about helping you live your best life I have created a free seven-day video training series where I walk you through some key steps that will help you fall in love with yourself, your body and your life. You can get access to this free video training series at www.paulagalli.com.

I look forward to helping you fall in love with yourself, your body and your life today.